ARTISTIC ADVENTURES

ROMANTIC VISIONS:

A COLORING BOOK FOR ADULTS

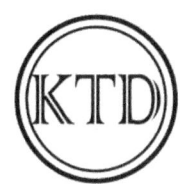 **KATE TAYLOR DESIGN**

I0479467

This book features 40 intricate illustrations. Each illustration is printed on one side of the page, providing a convenient and enjoyable coloring experience for adults.

SCAN ME

If you would like to reorder, please scan the QR Code

ROMANTICISM

was an artistic and intellectual movement that originated in Europe during the late 18th century and lasted until the mid-19th century. It was characterized by an emphasis on emotion, individualism, and the imagination. Romantic artists sought to express their own feelings and ideas through their work, often exploring themes of nature, mysticism, and the supernatural. The movement was marked by a rejection of the Enlightenment's emphasis on reason and rationality, and instead celebrated the irrational, the mysterious, and the sublime.

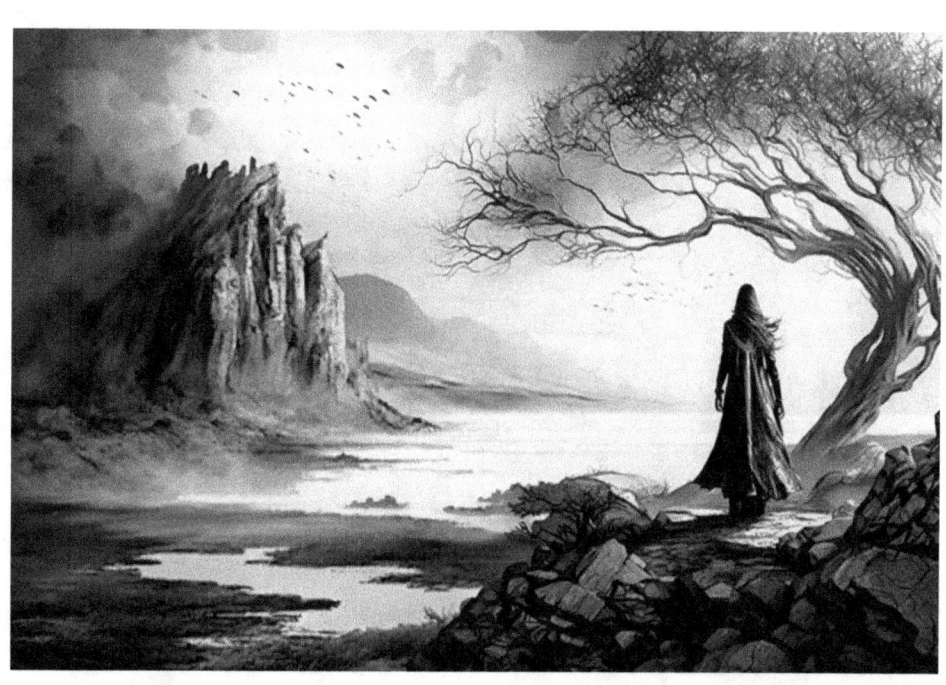

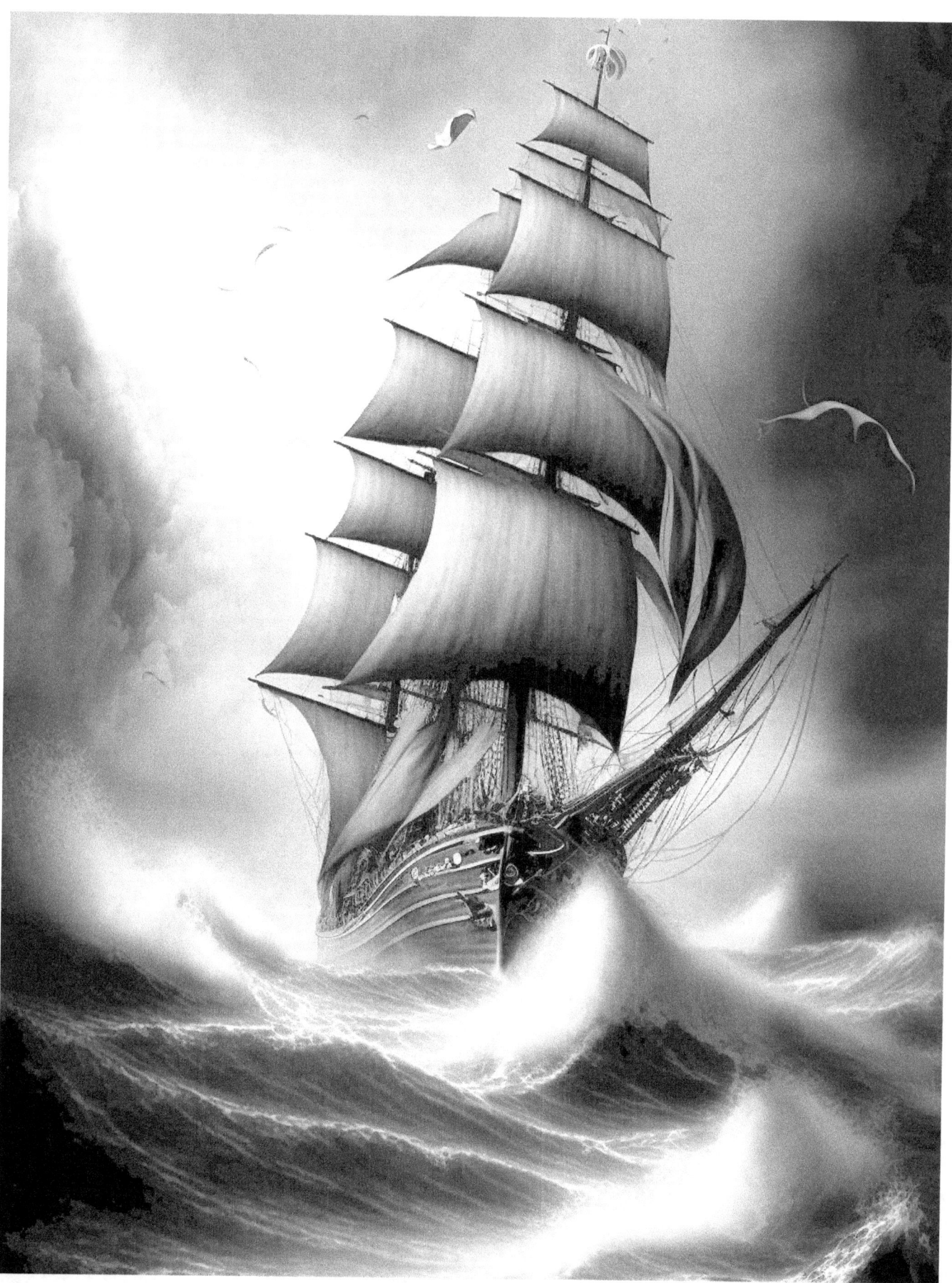

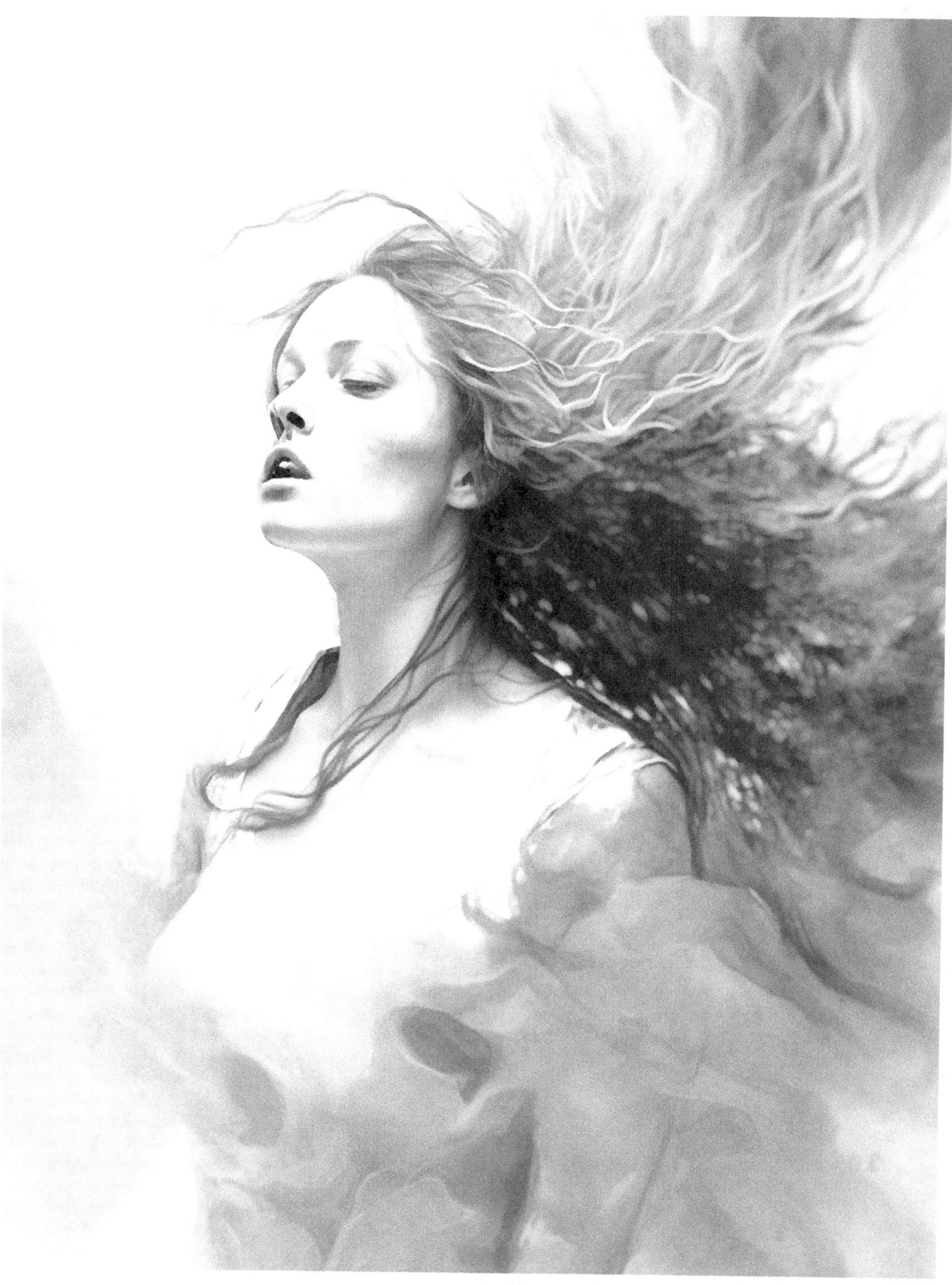

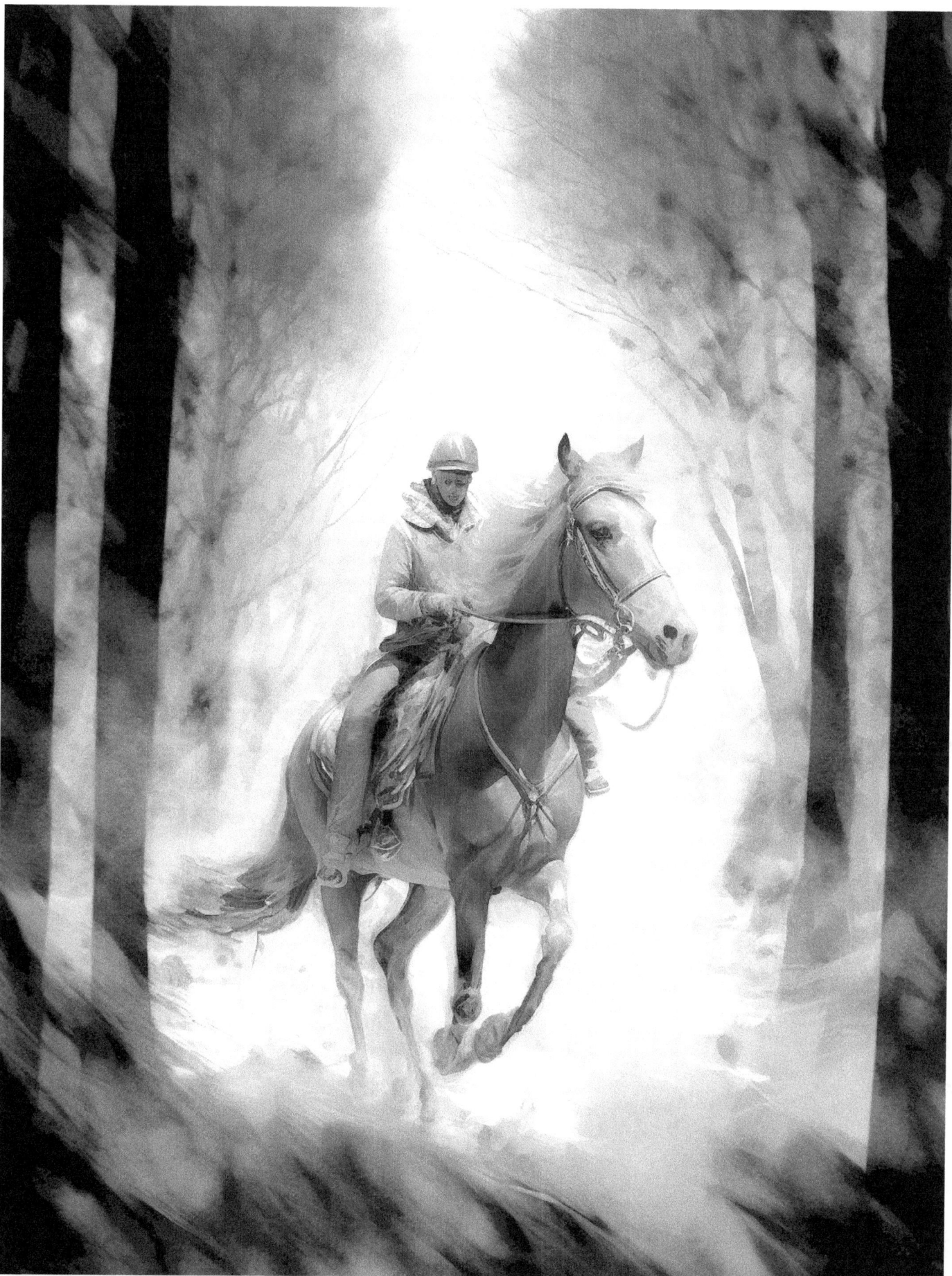

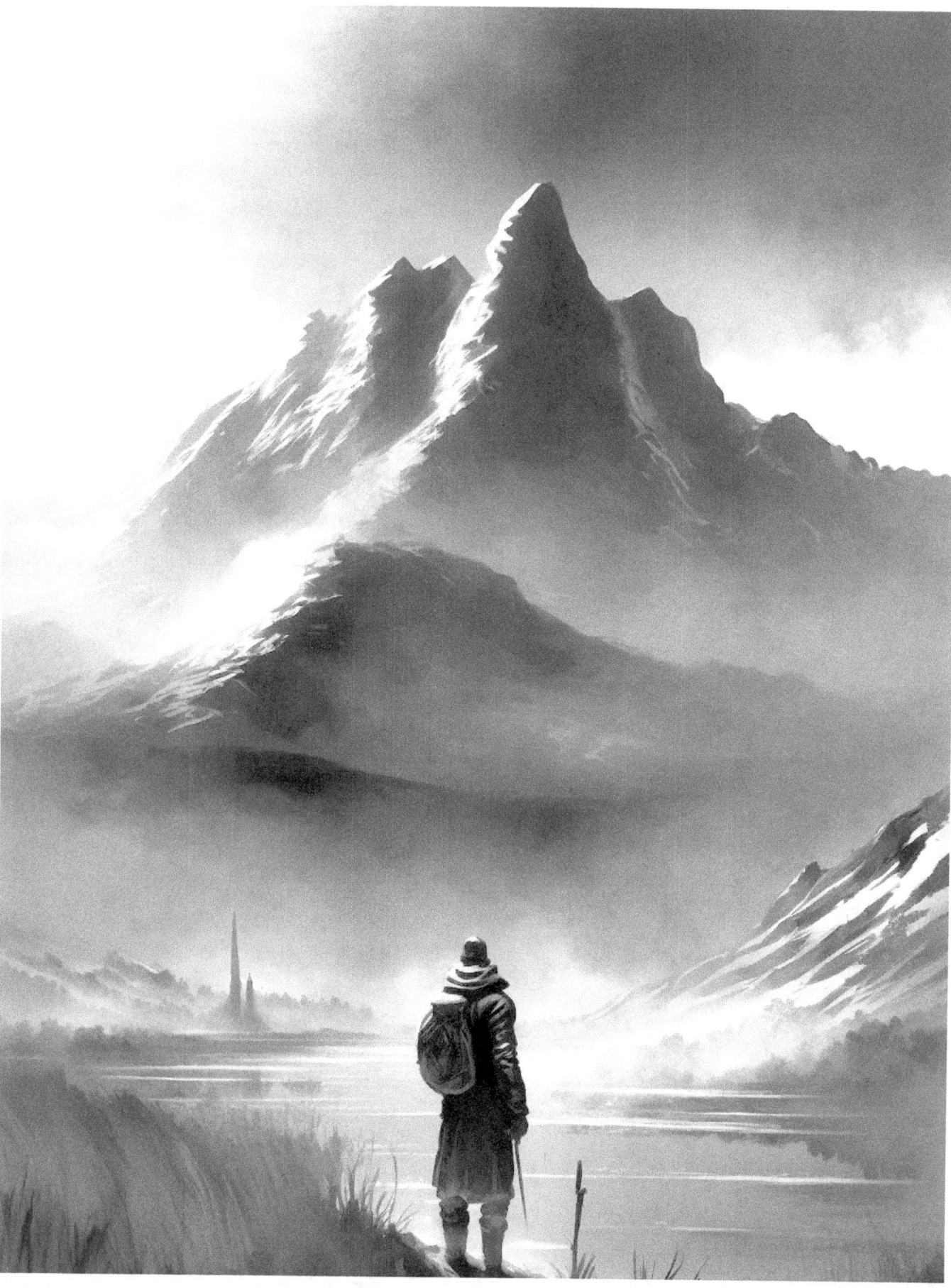

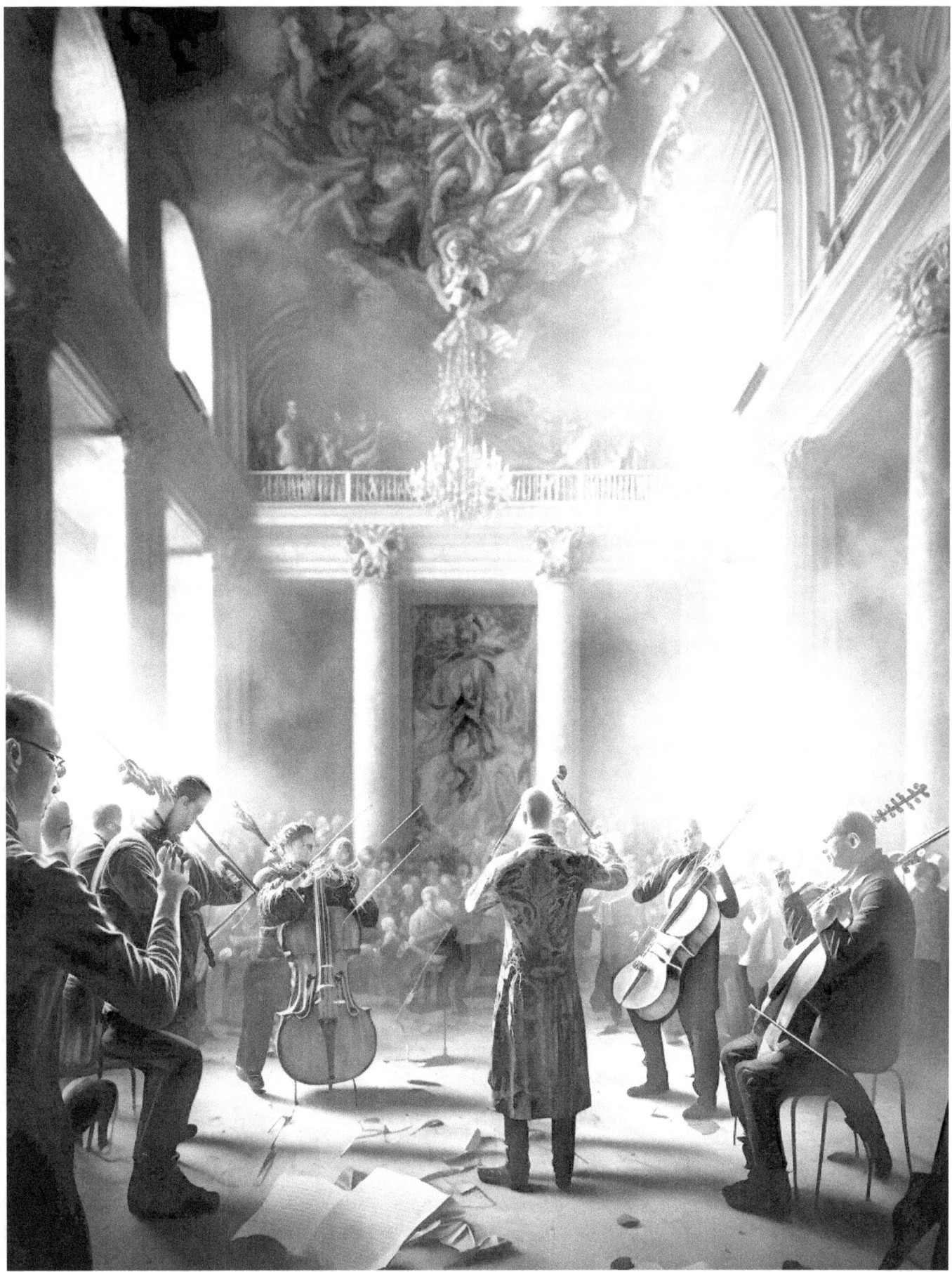

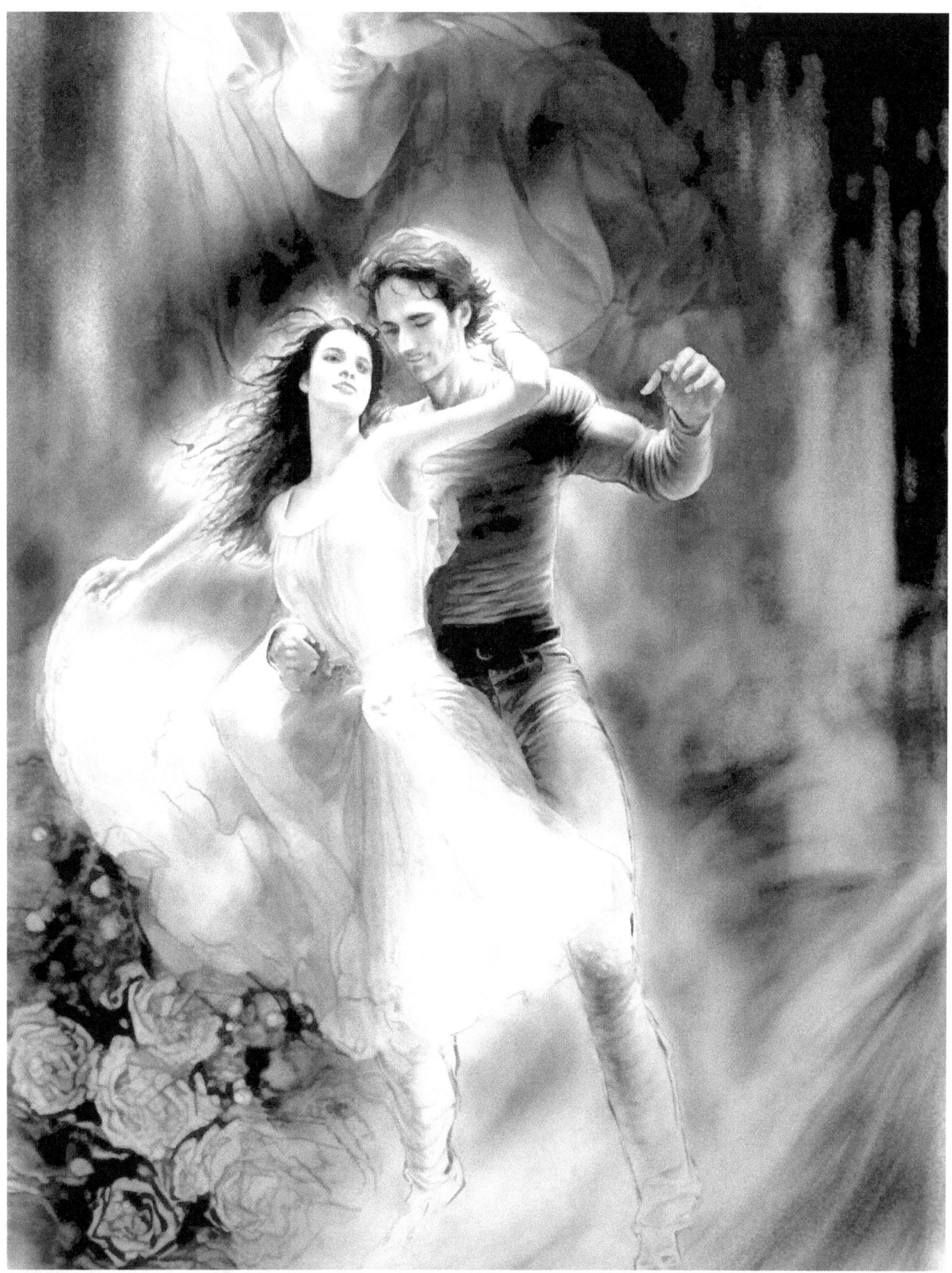

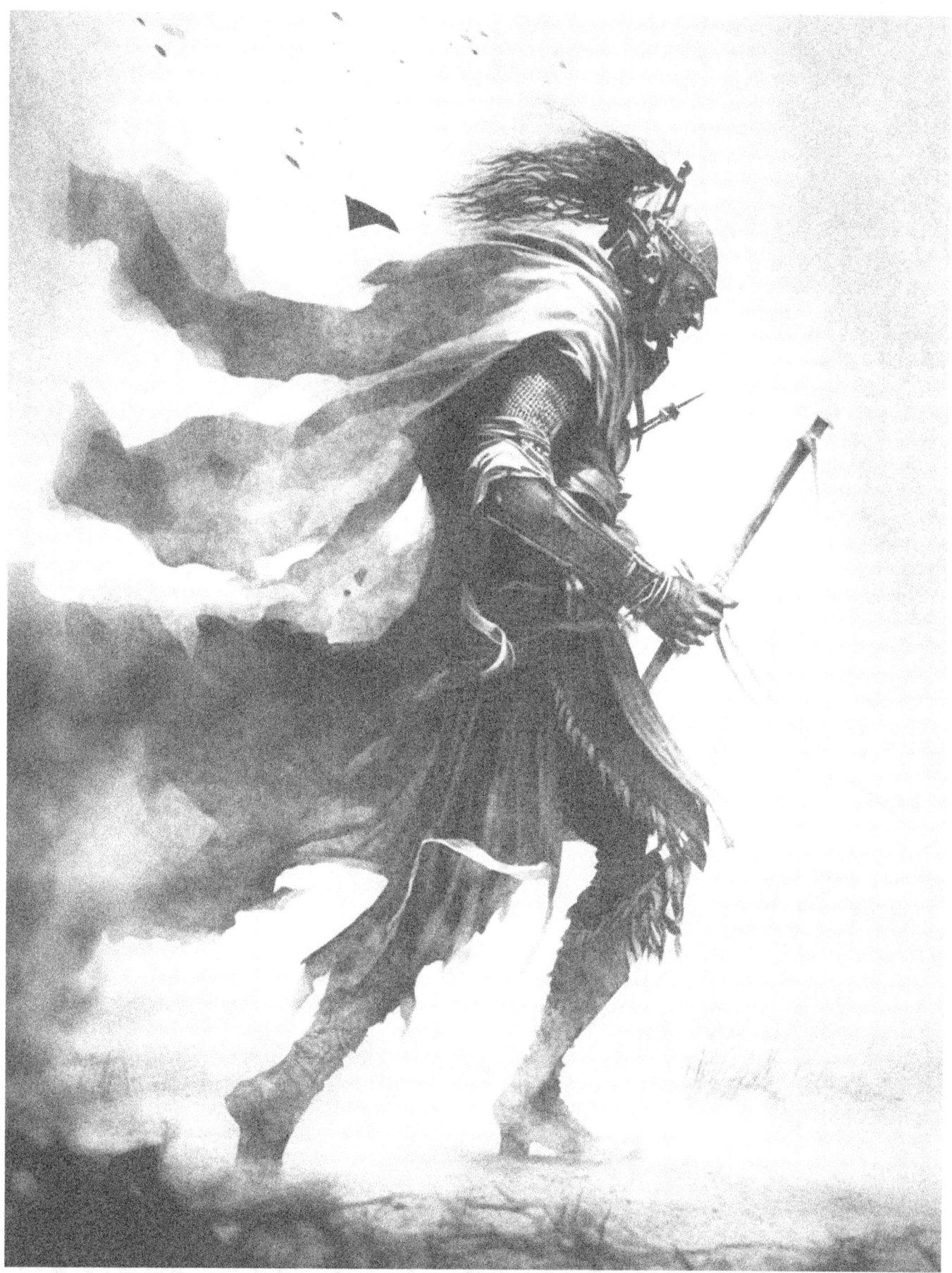

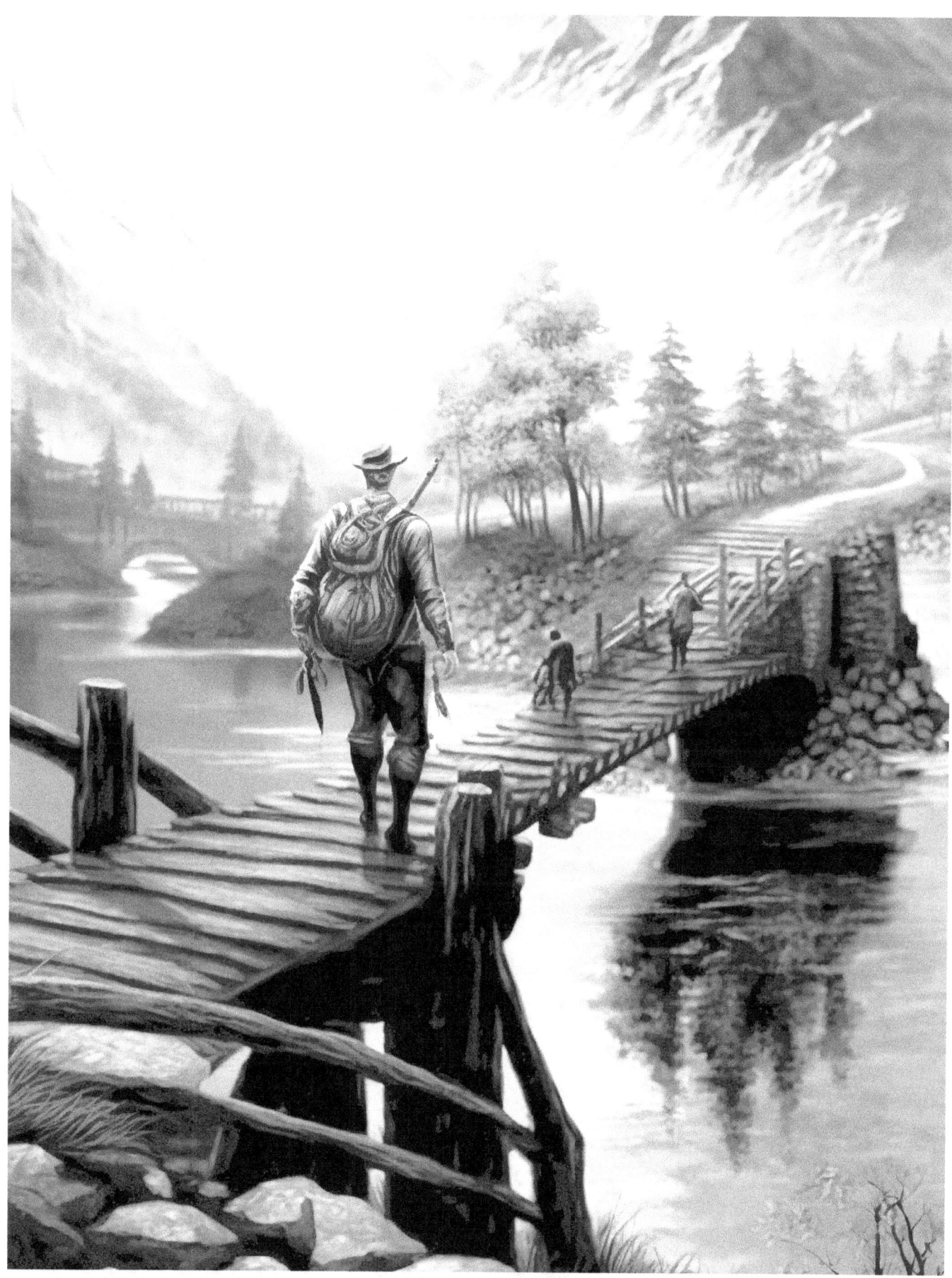

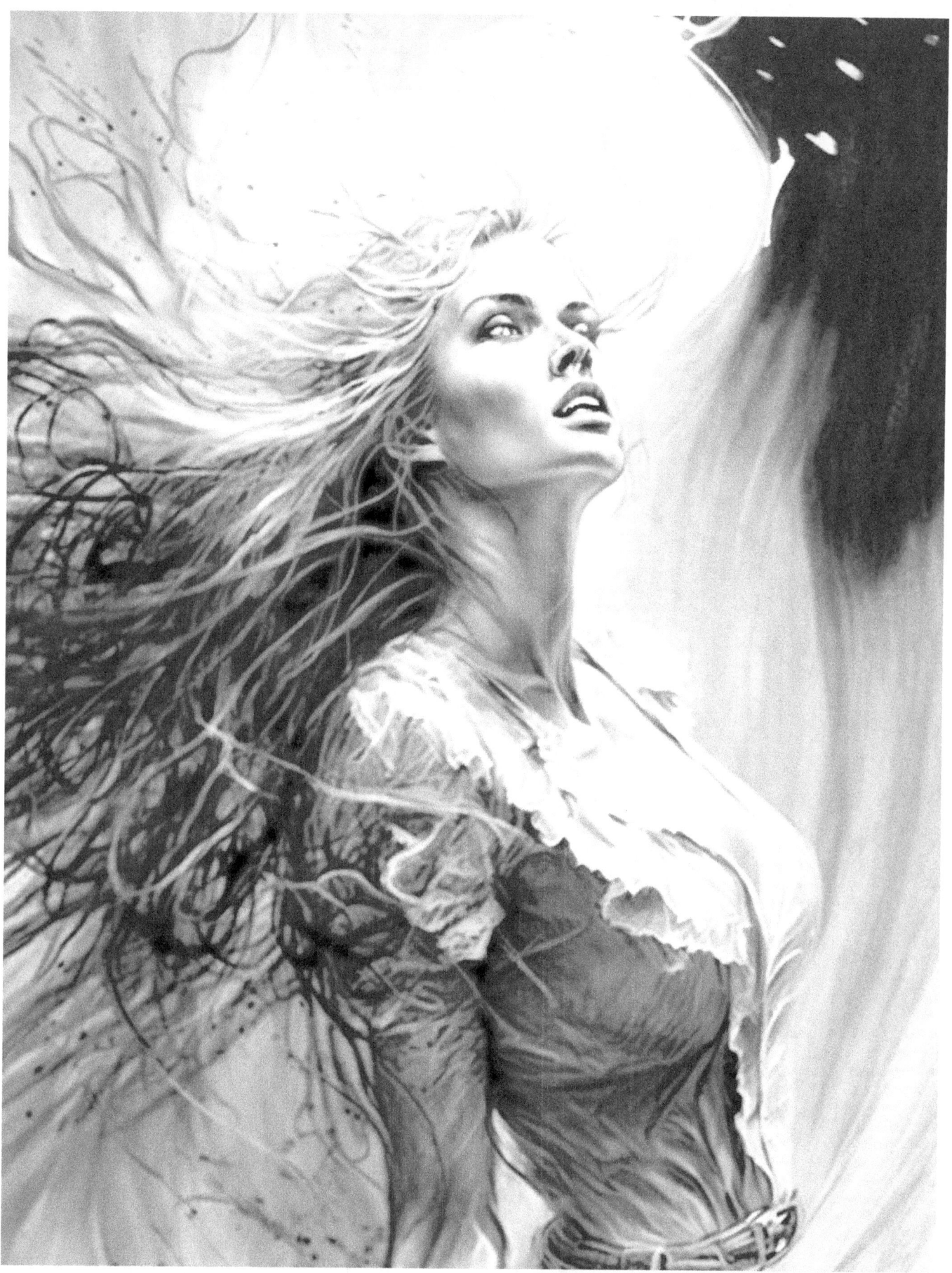

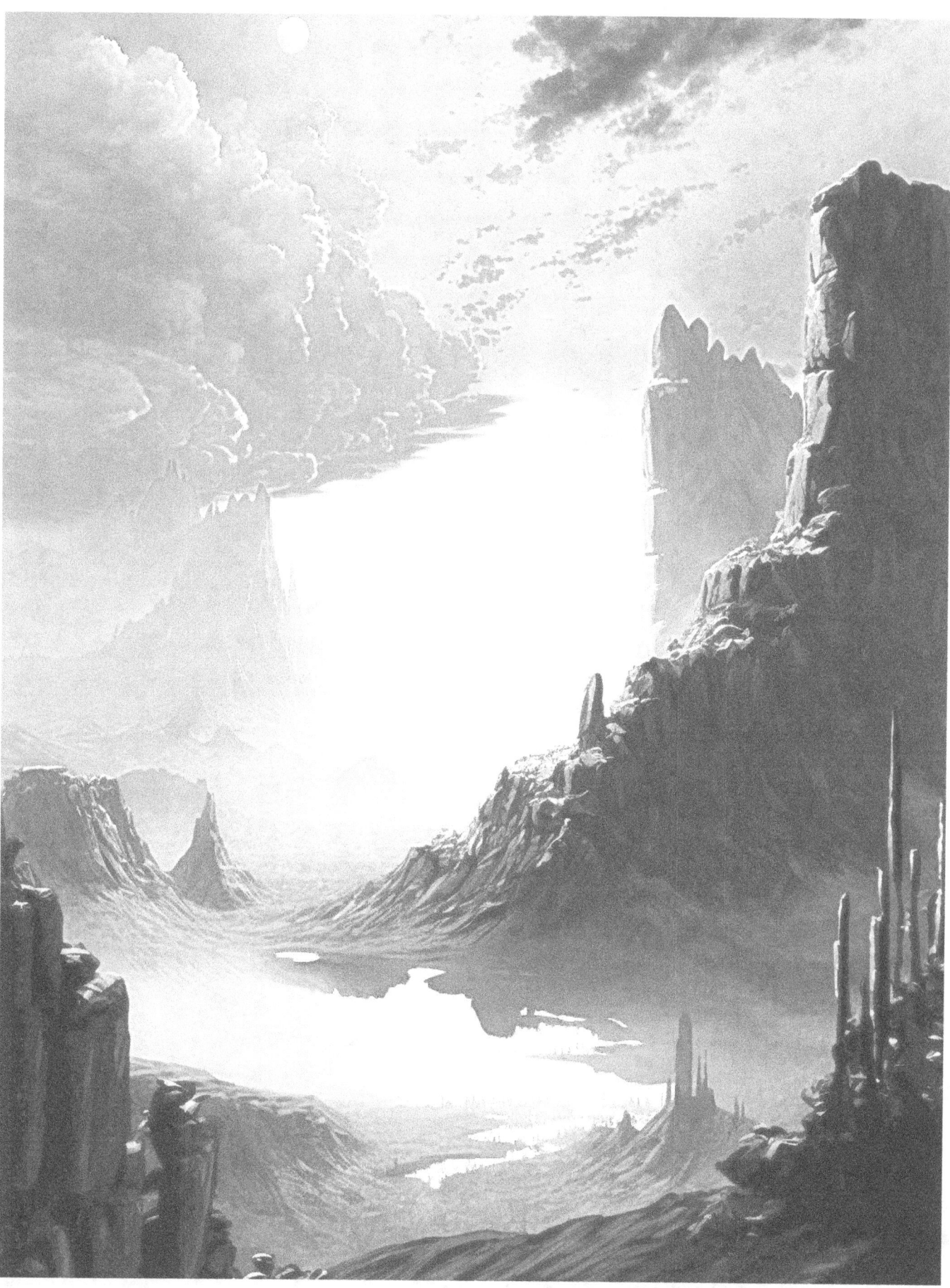

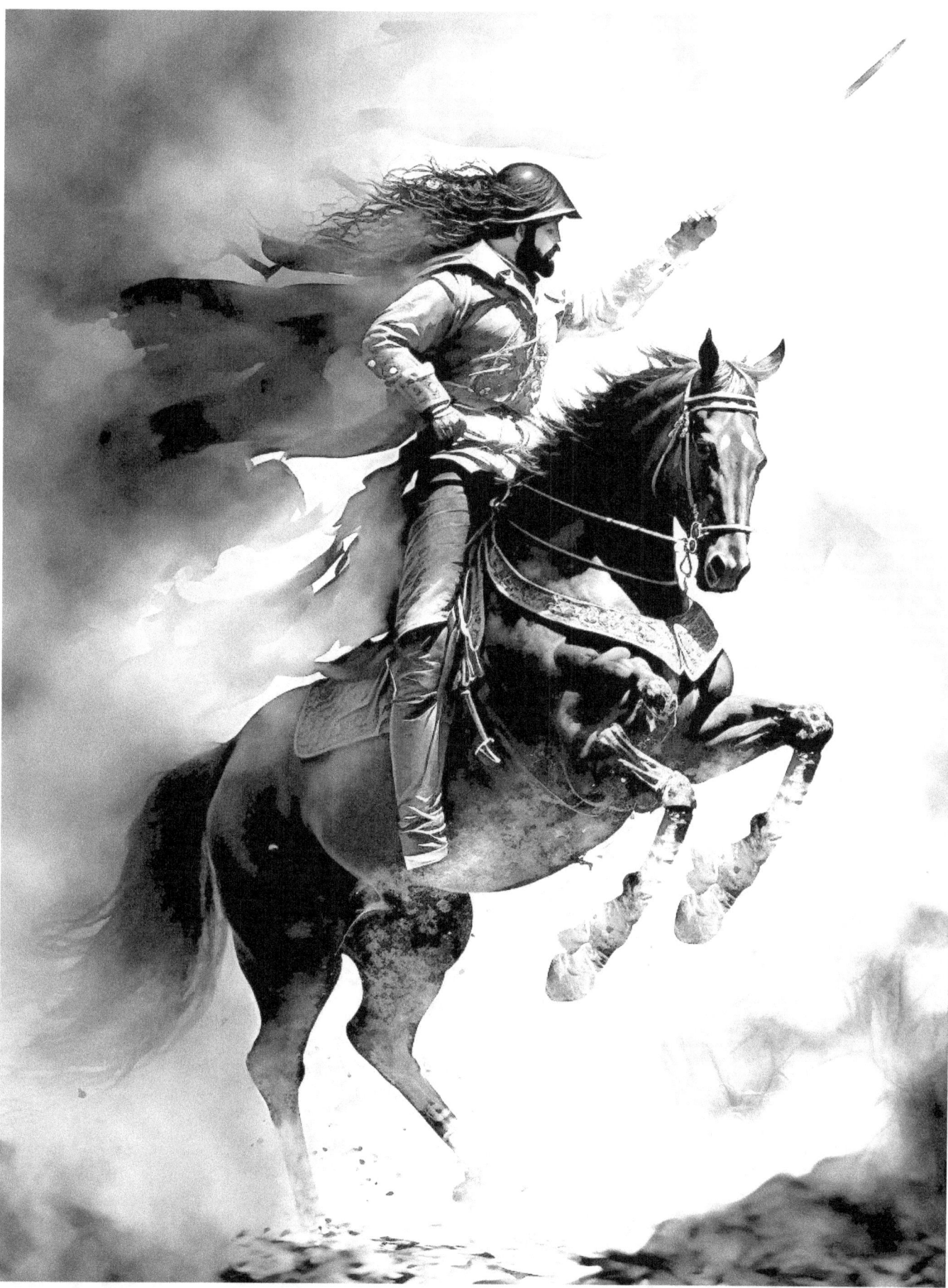

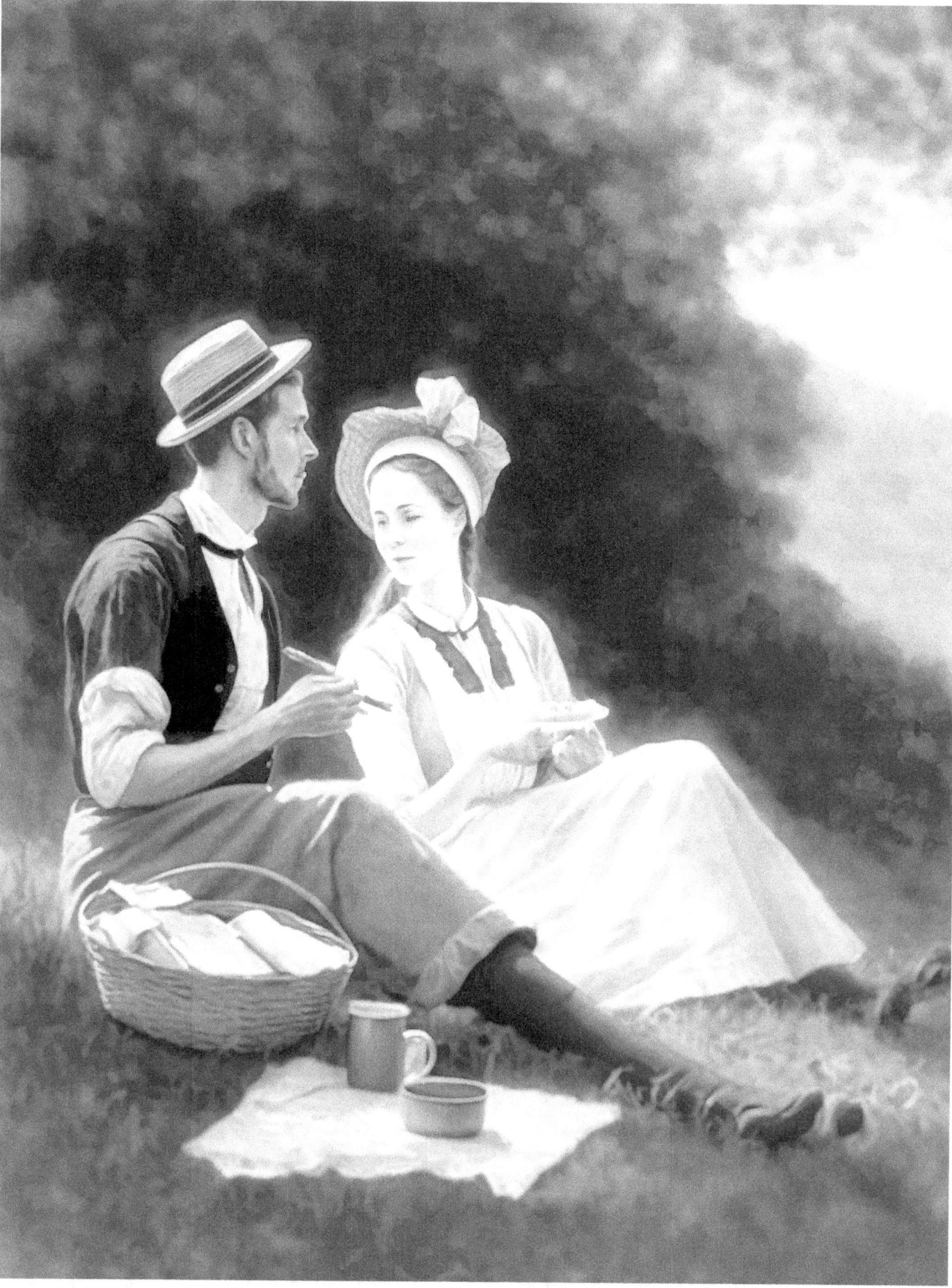

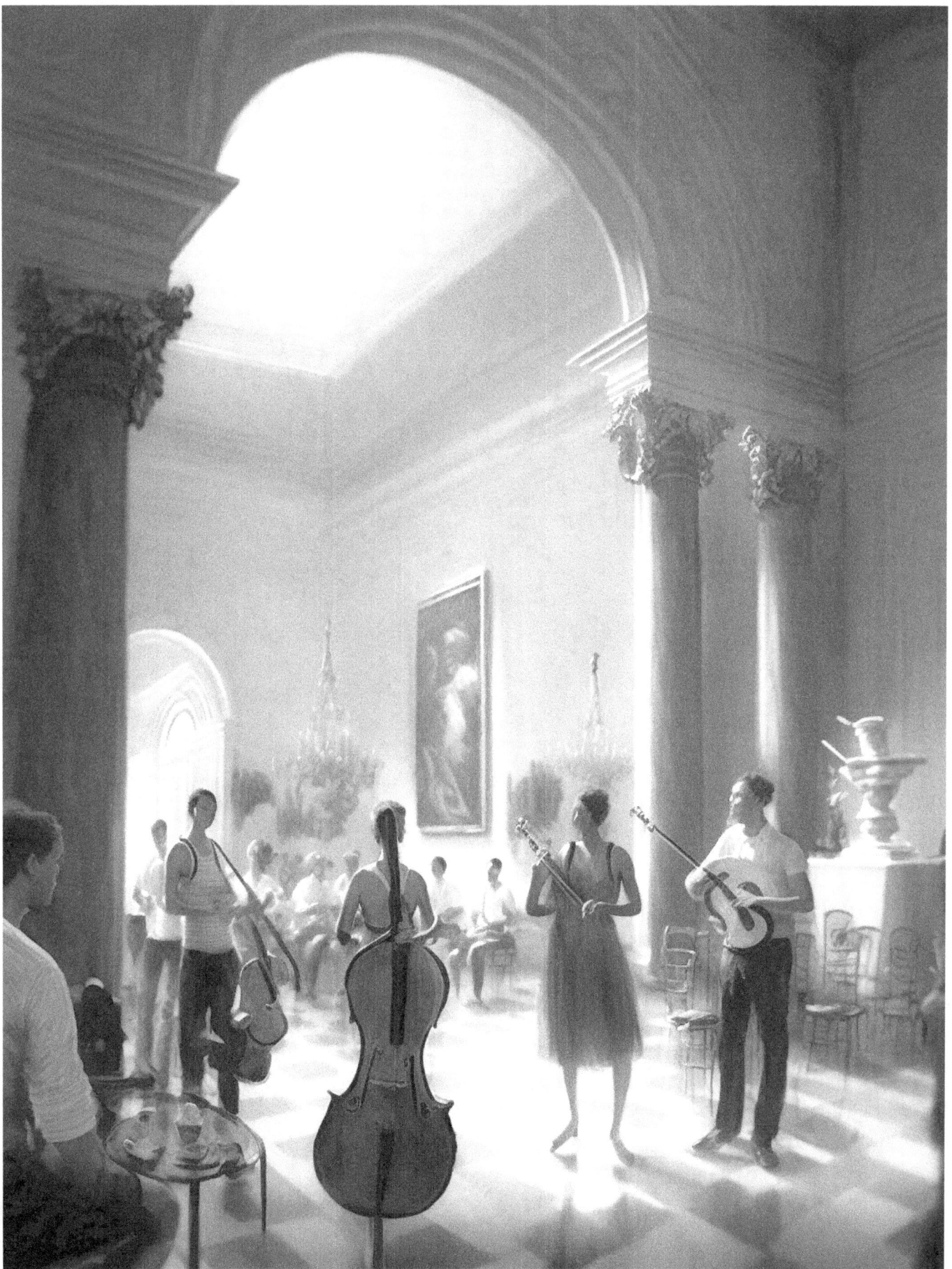

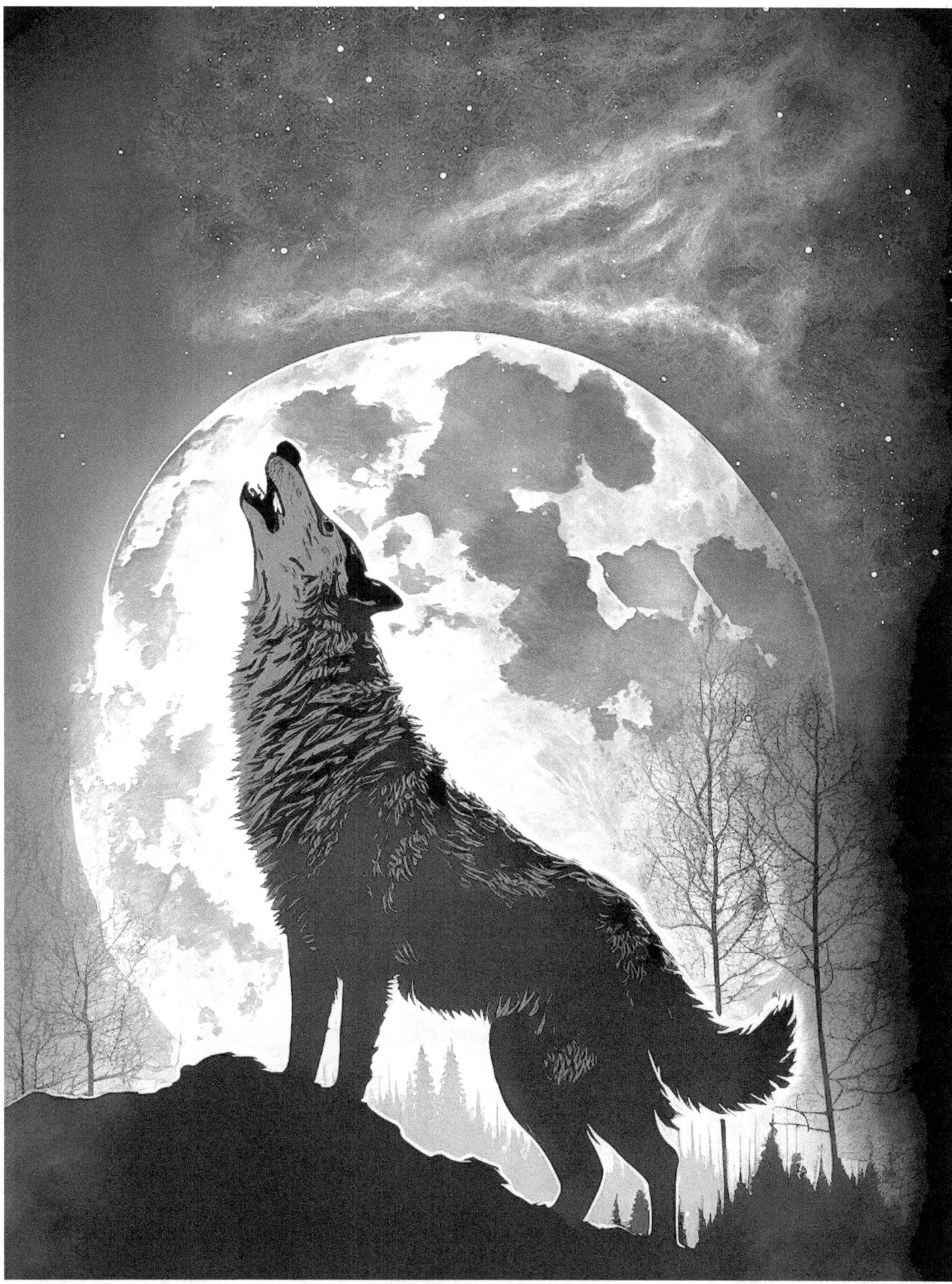

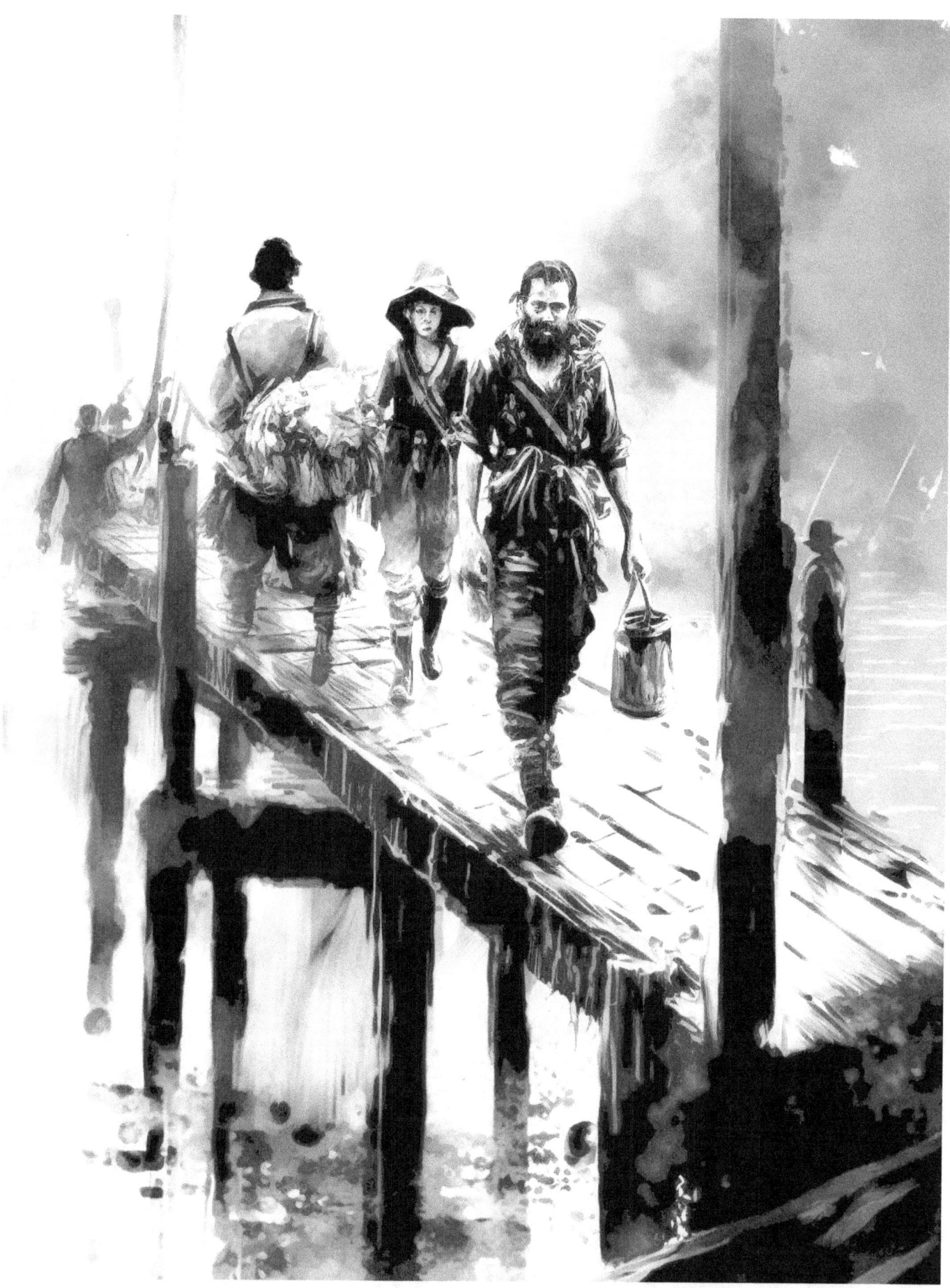

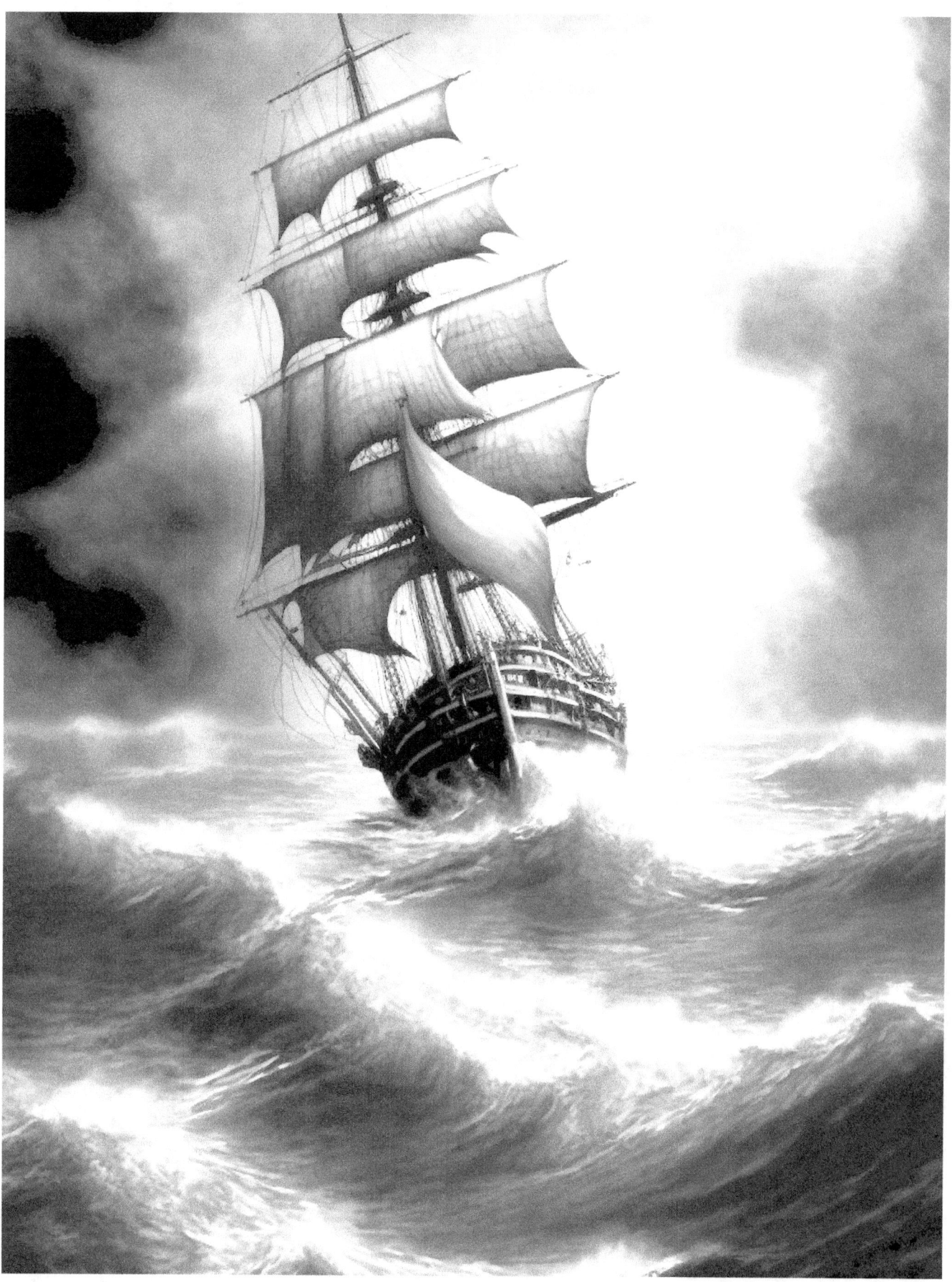

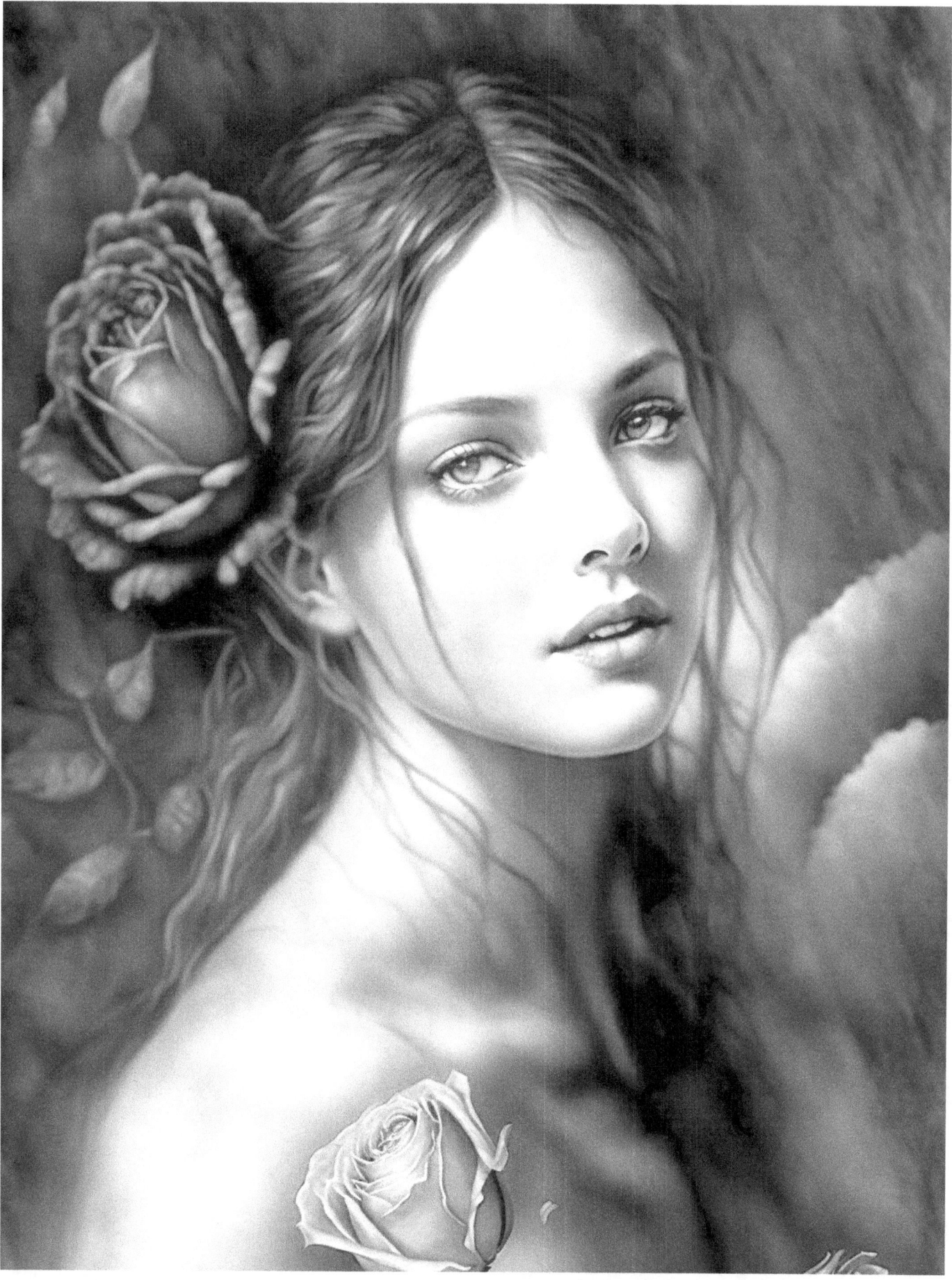

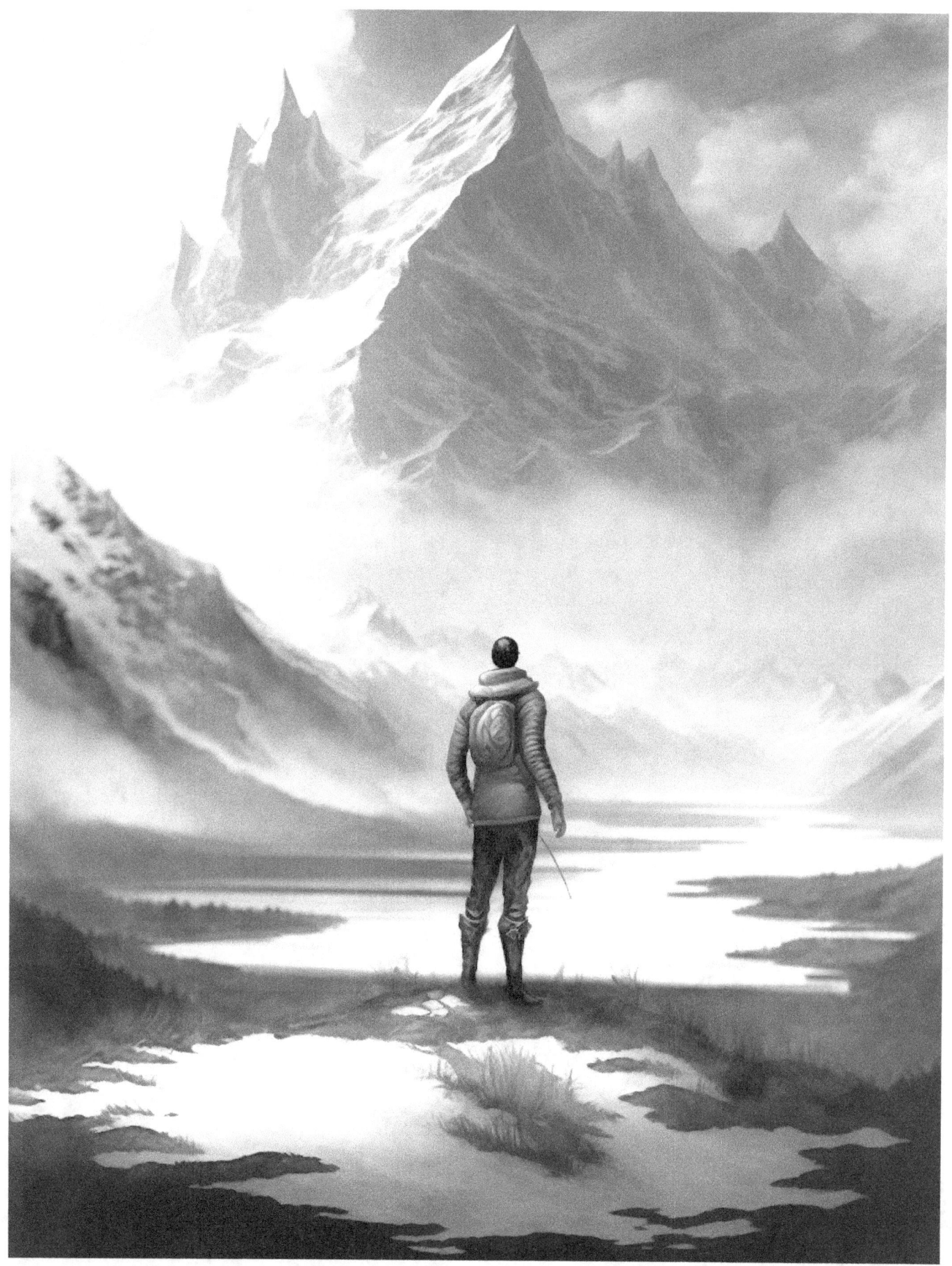

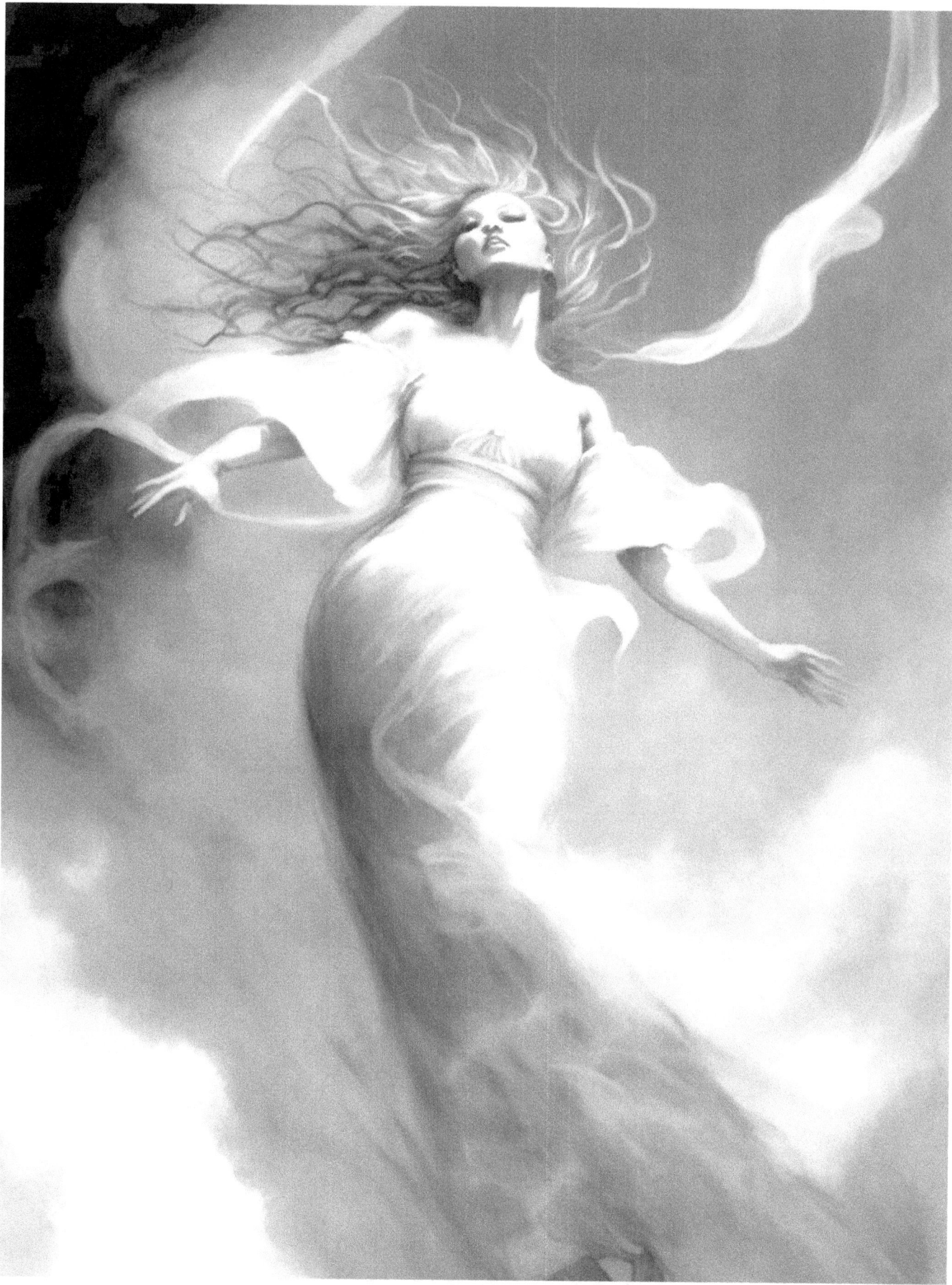

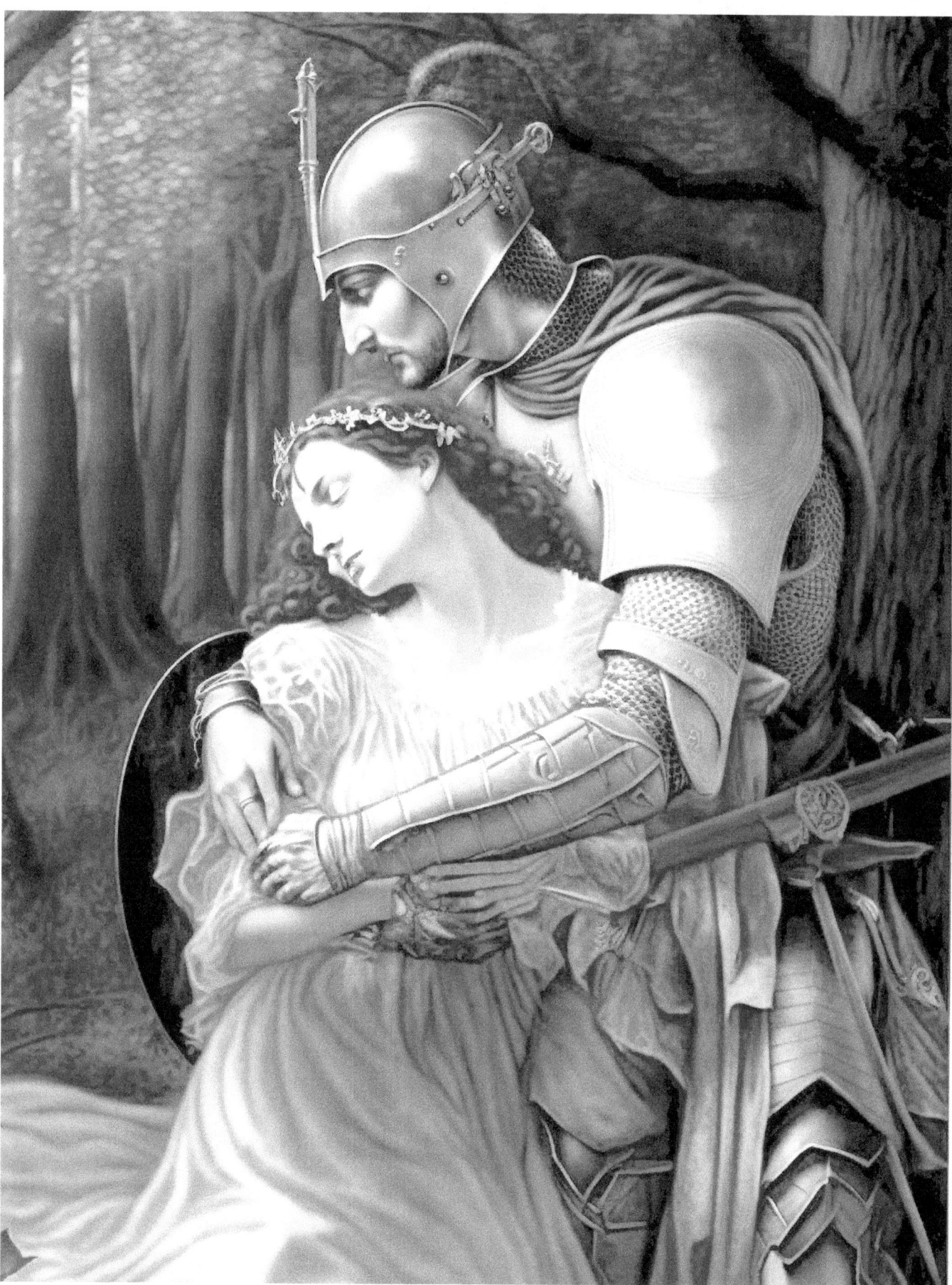

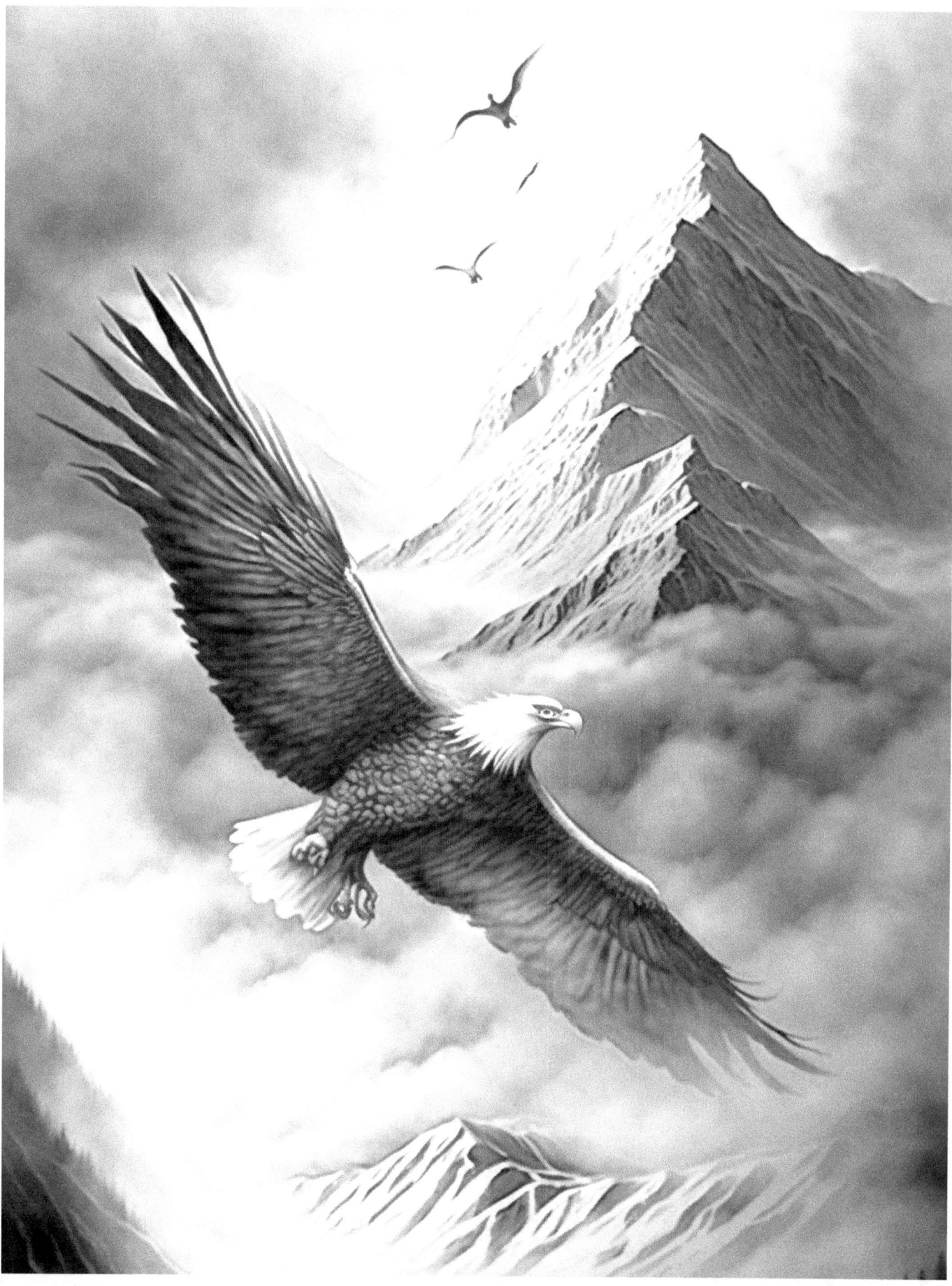

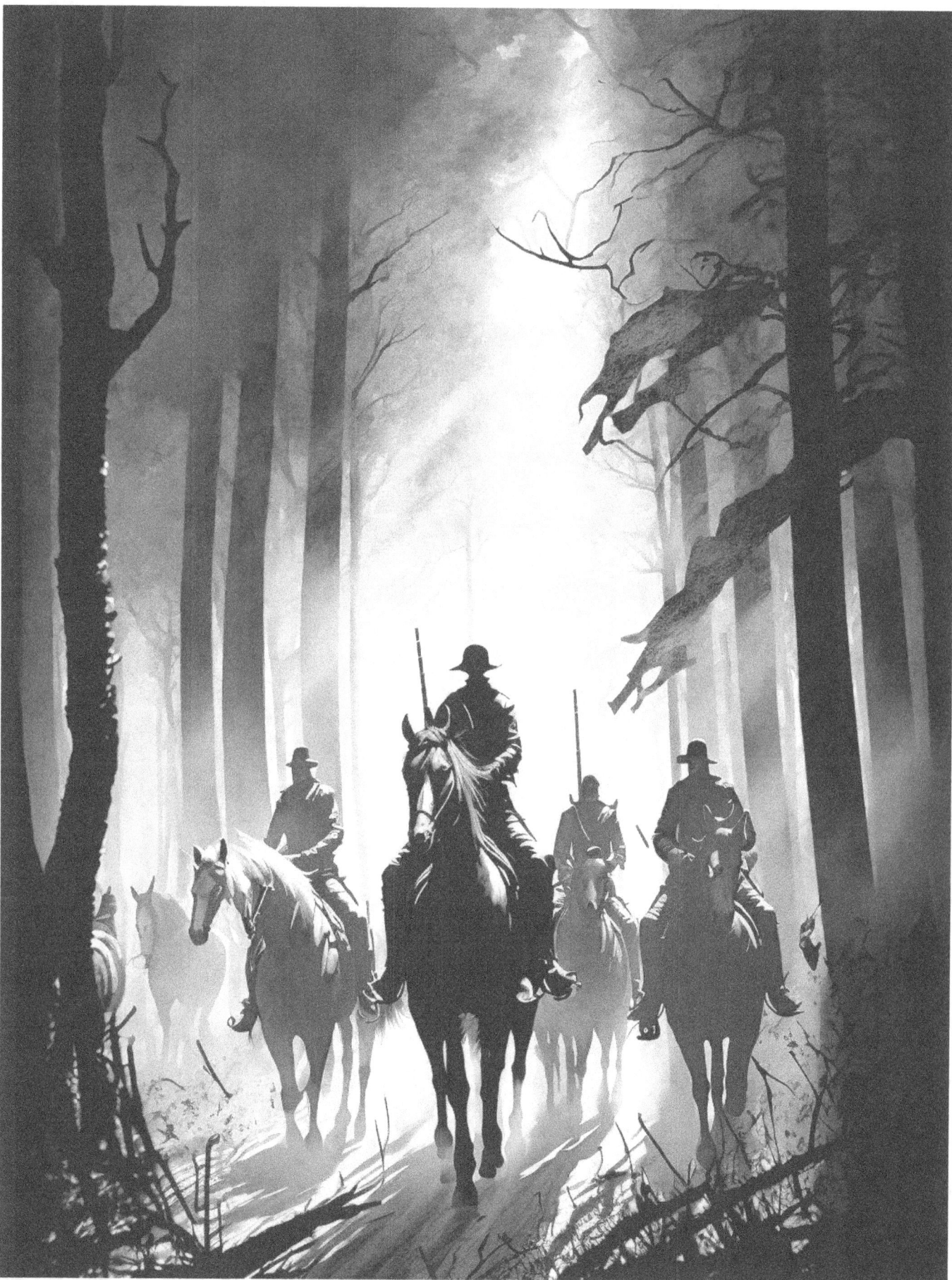

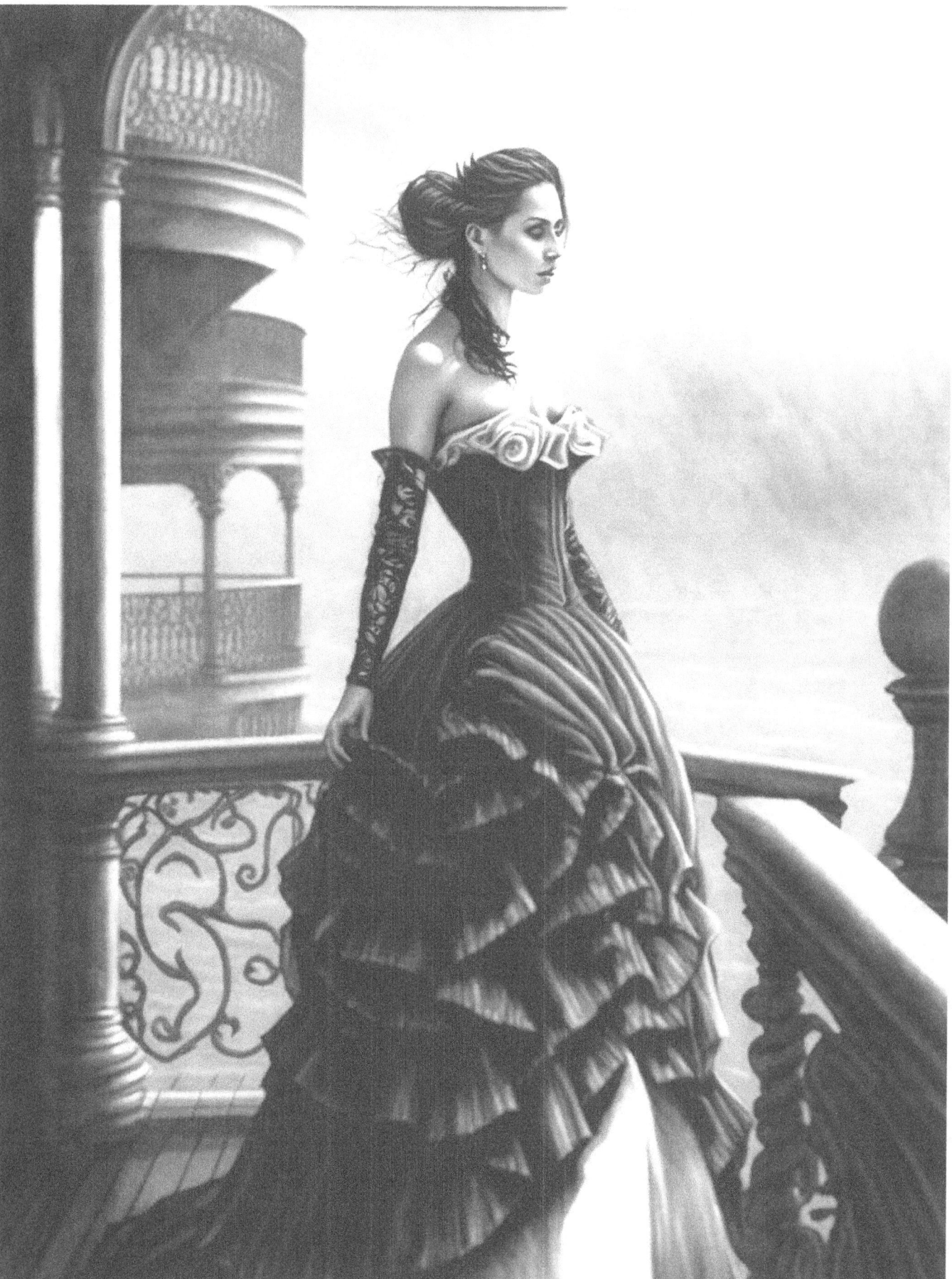

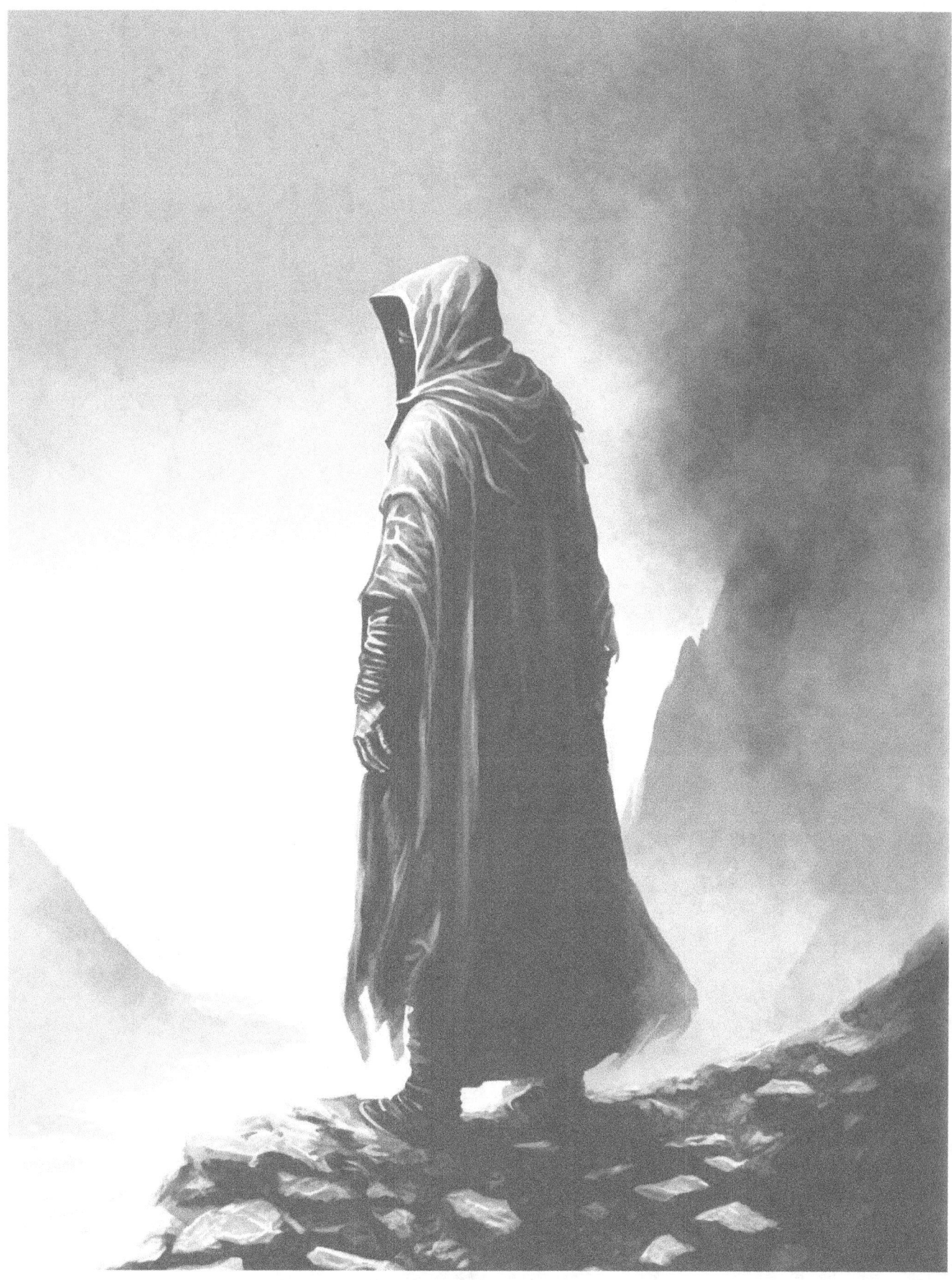

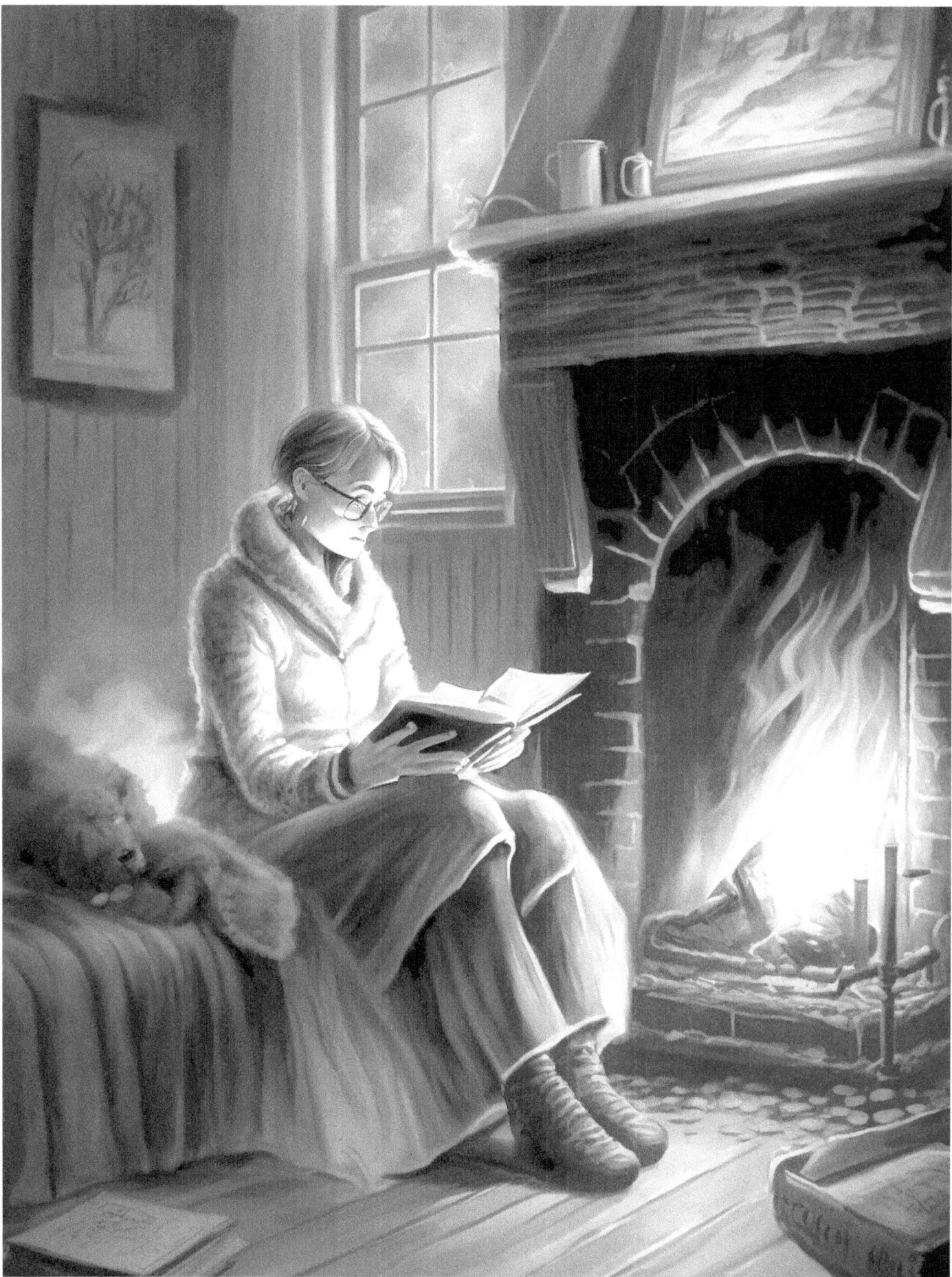

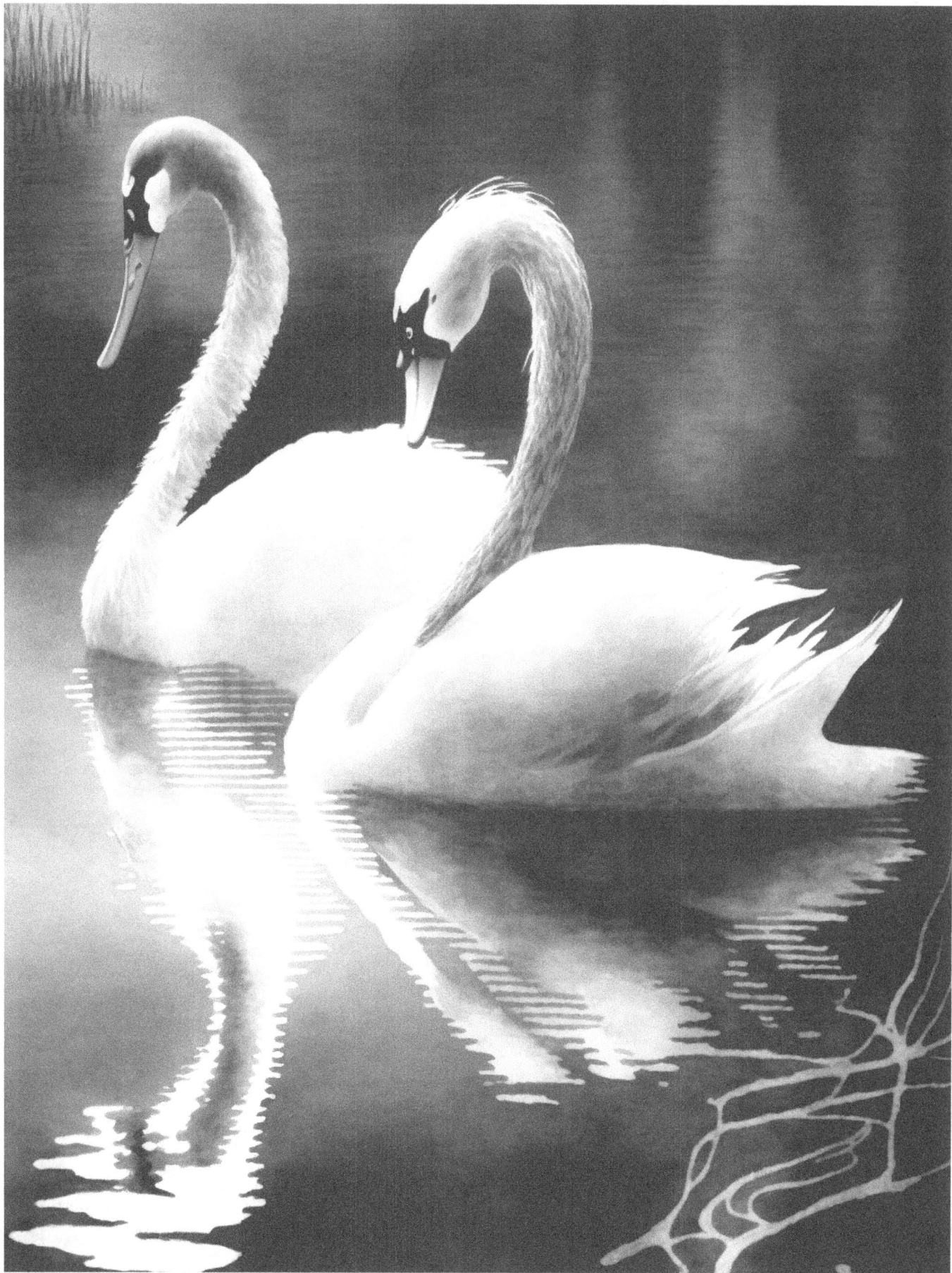

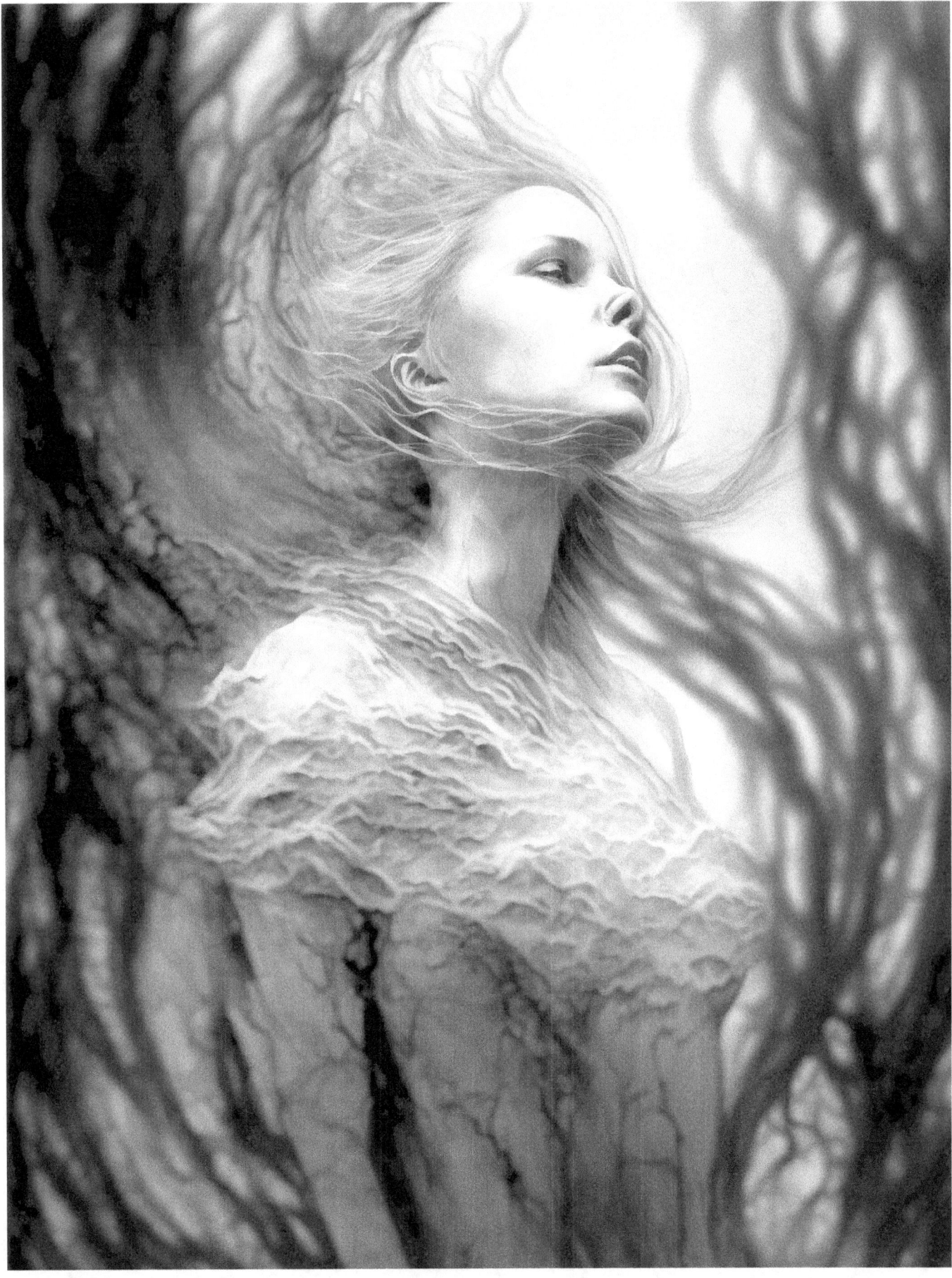

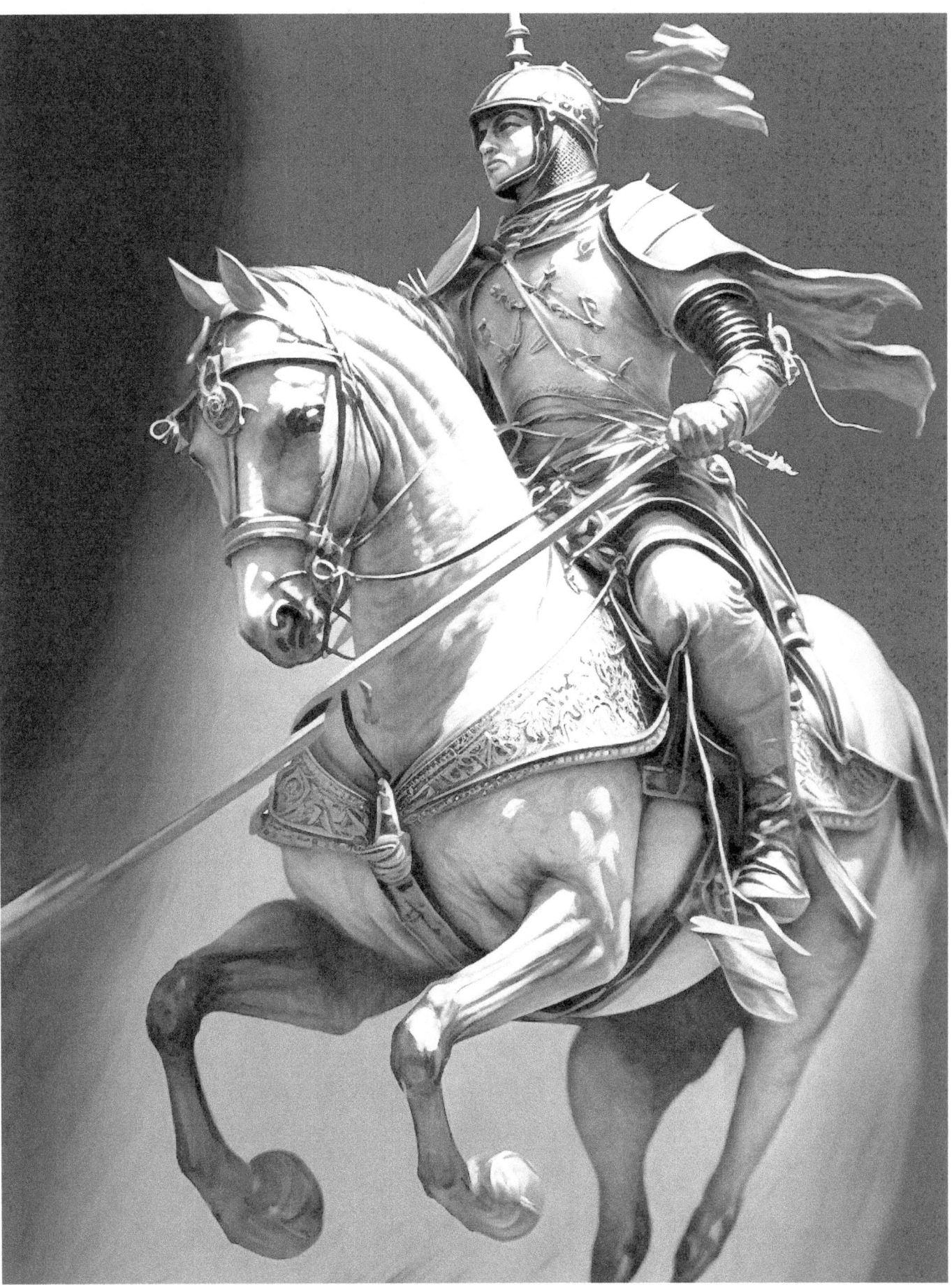

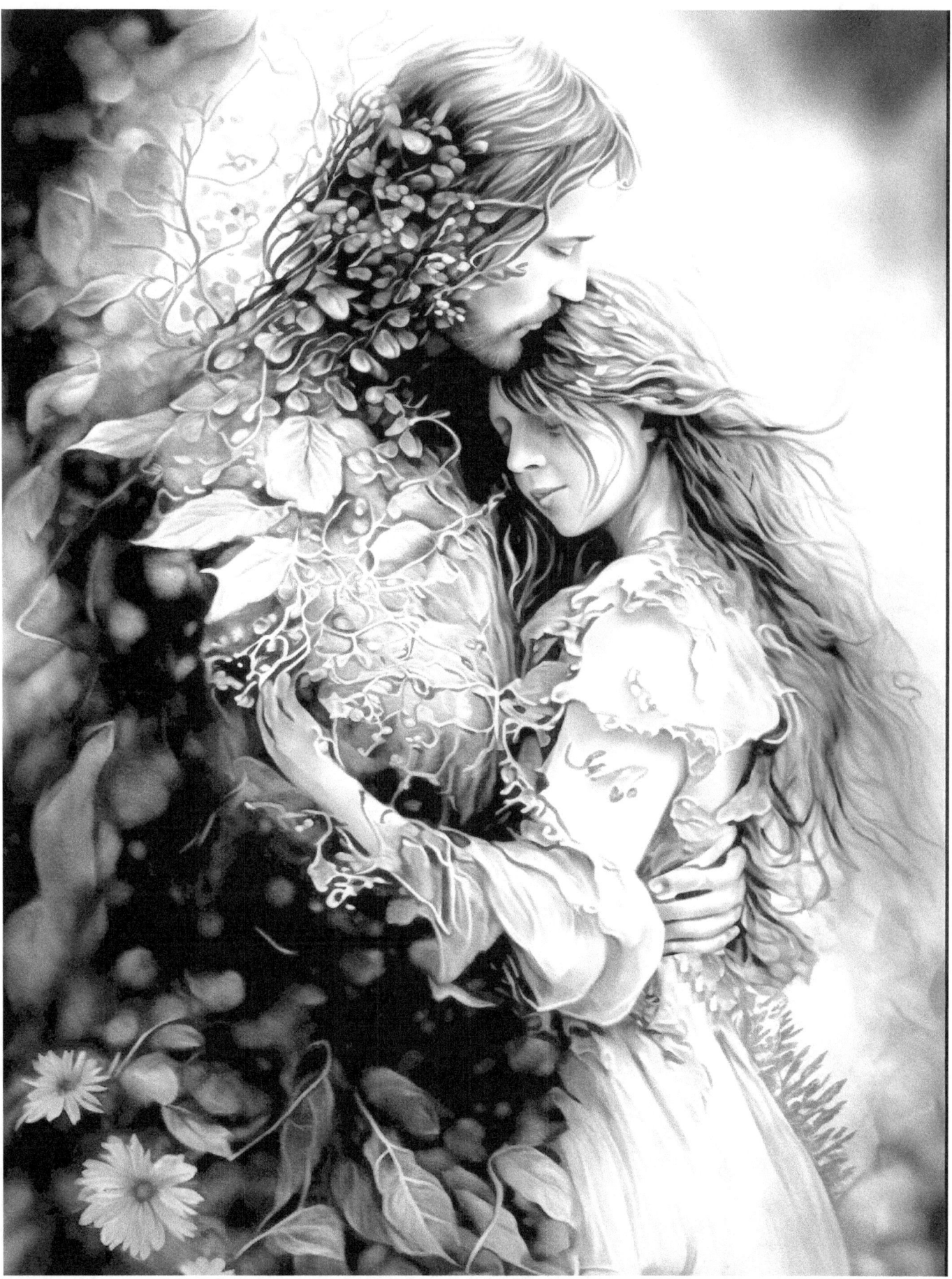

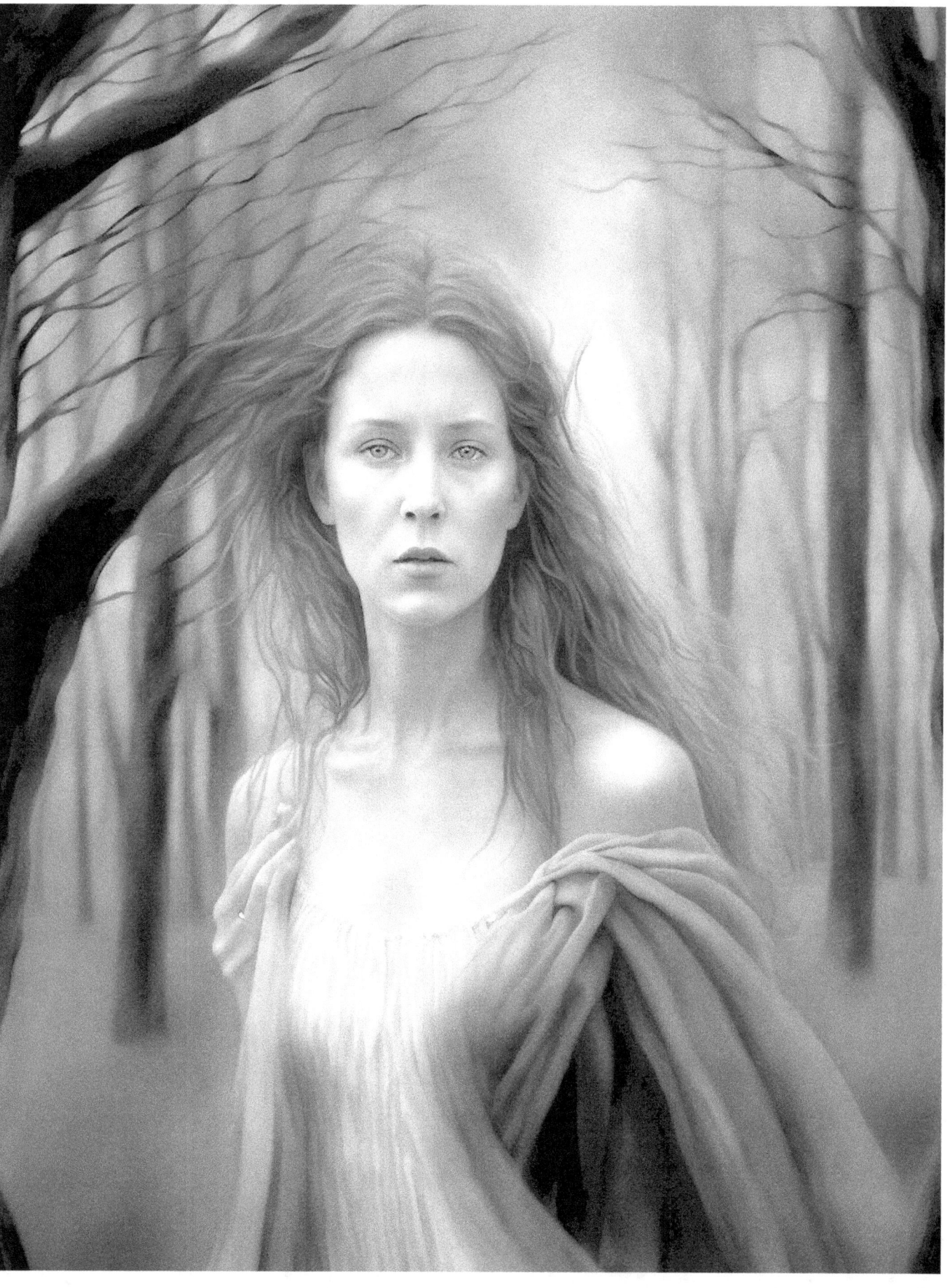

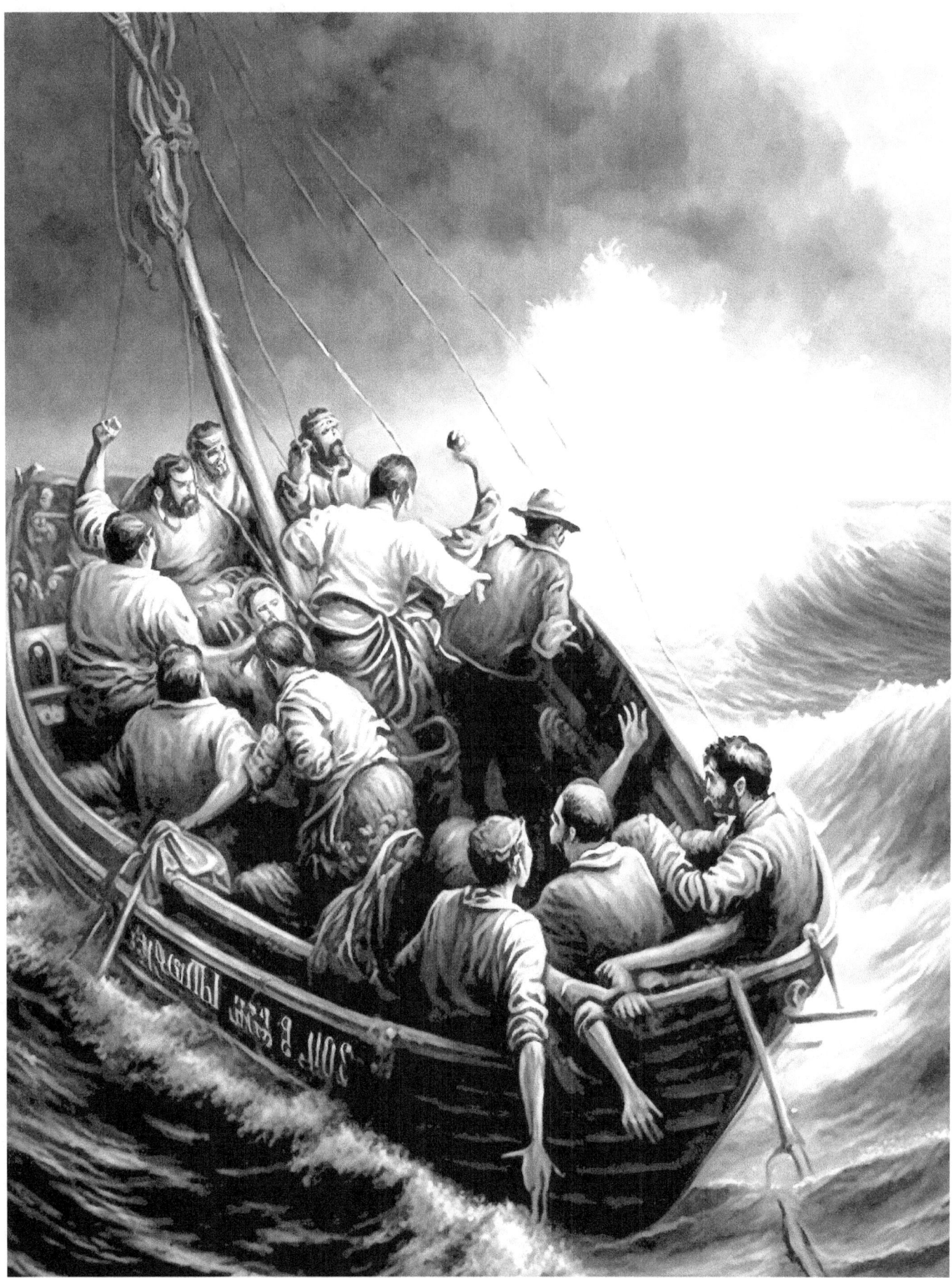

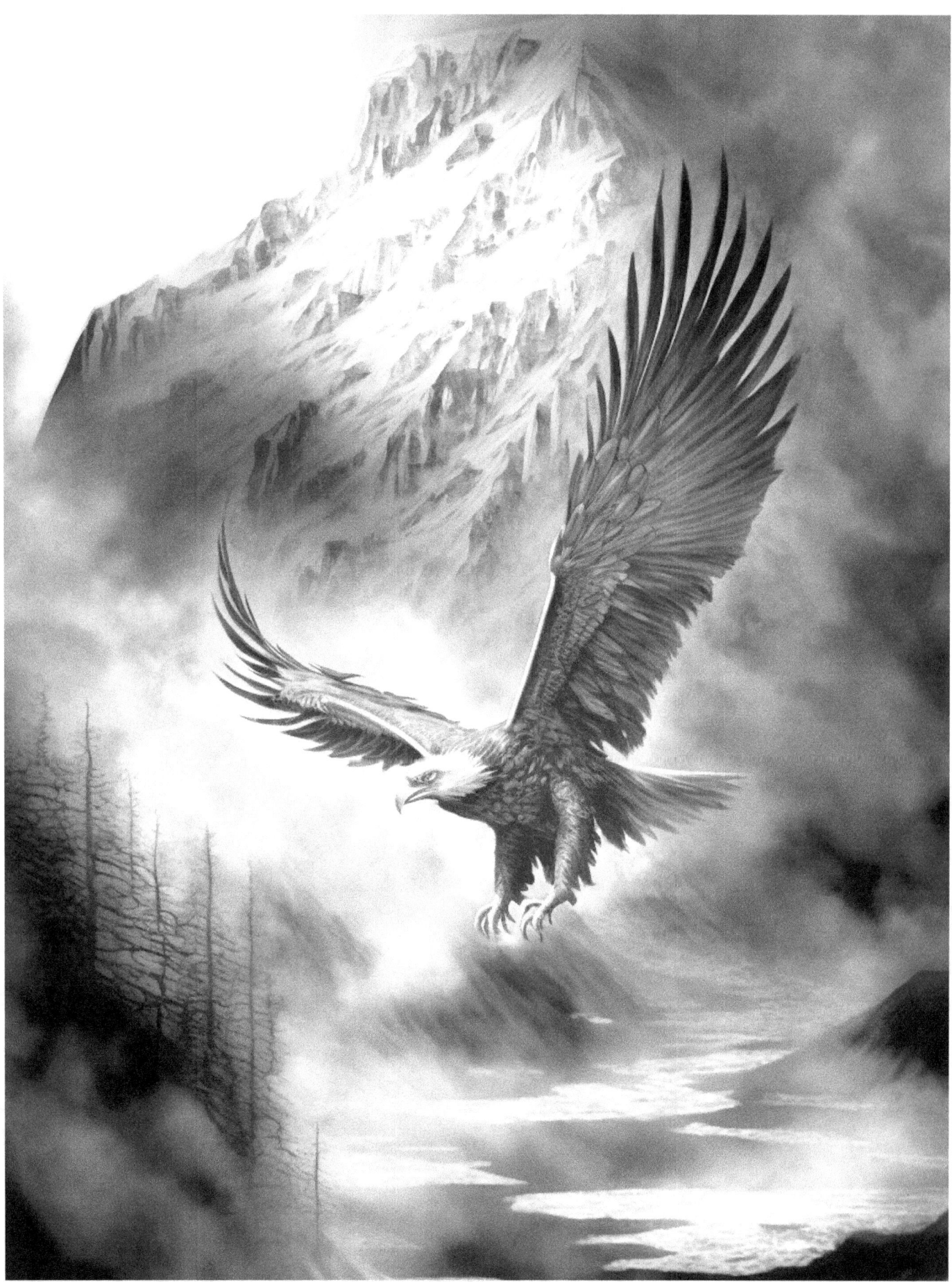

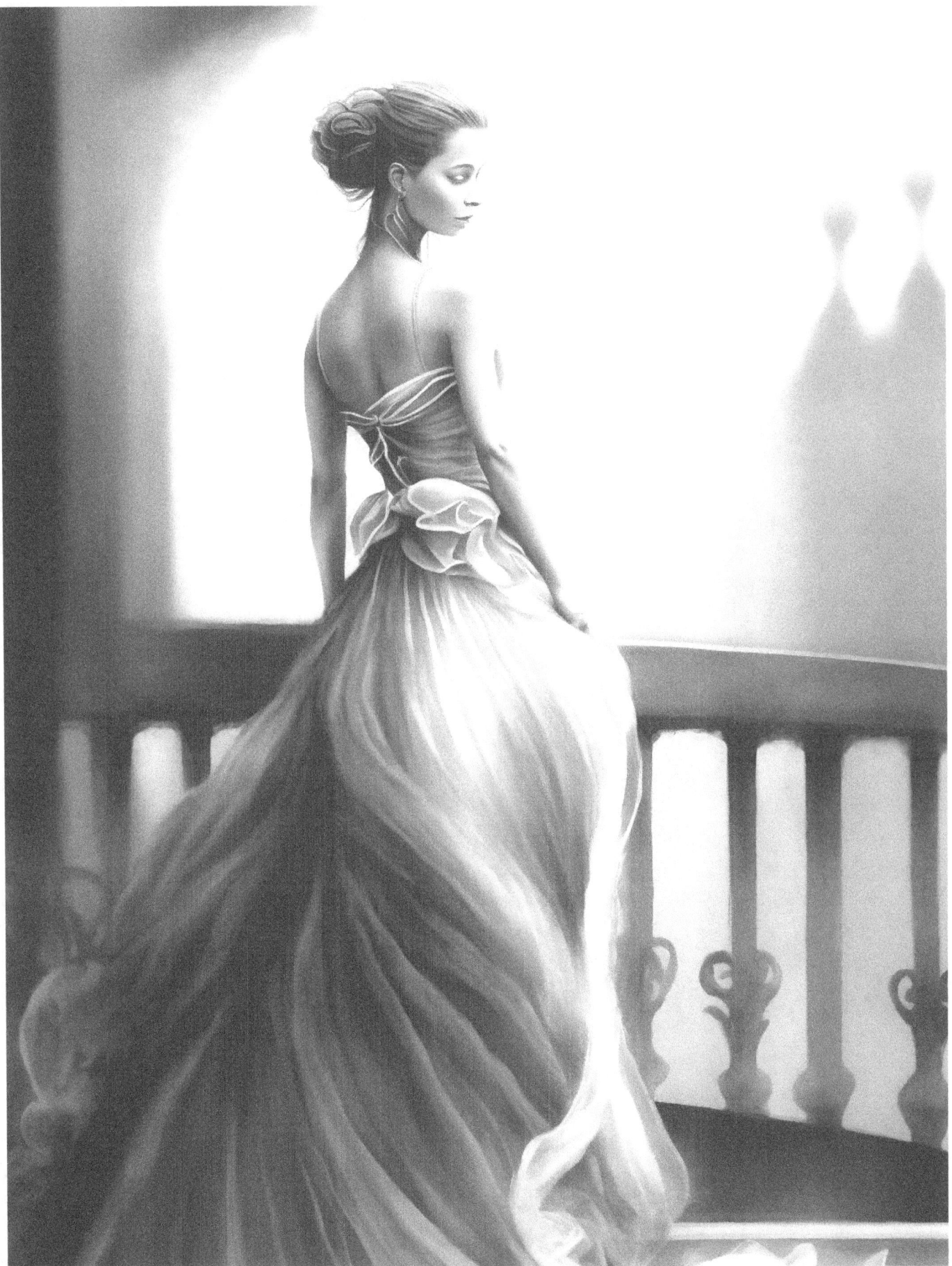

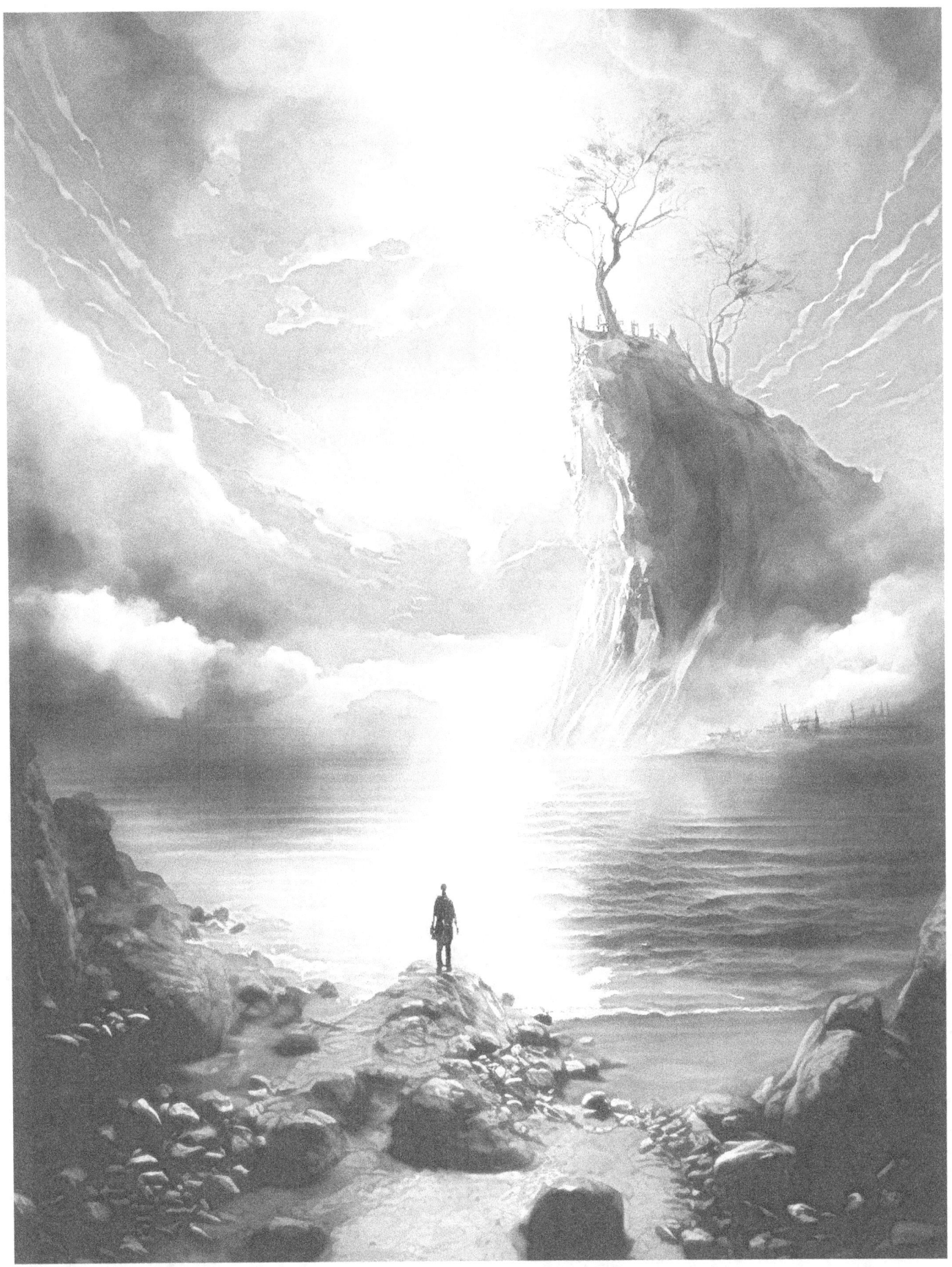

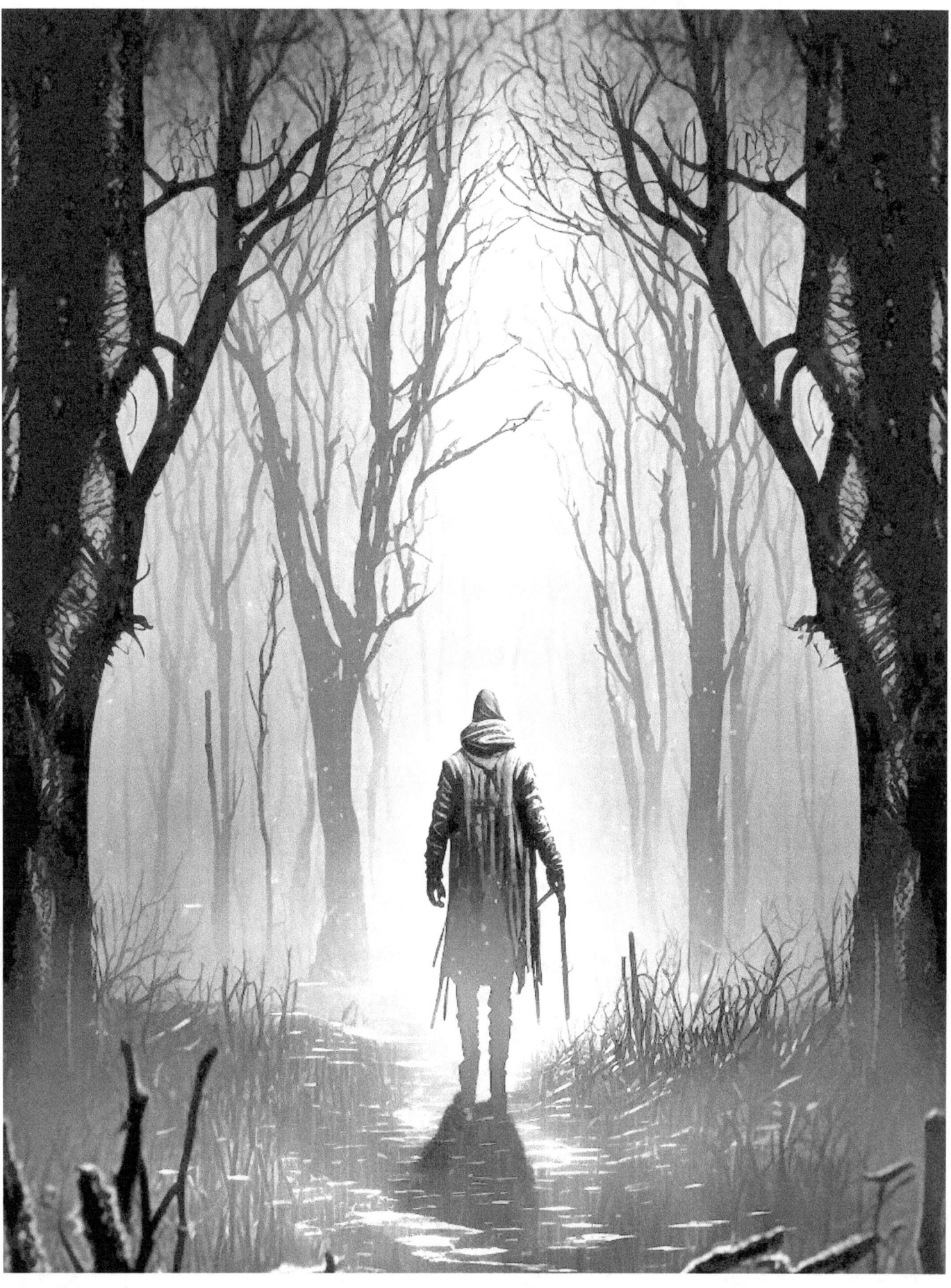

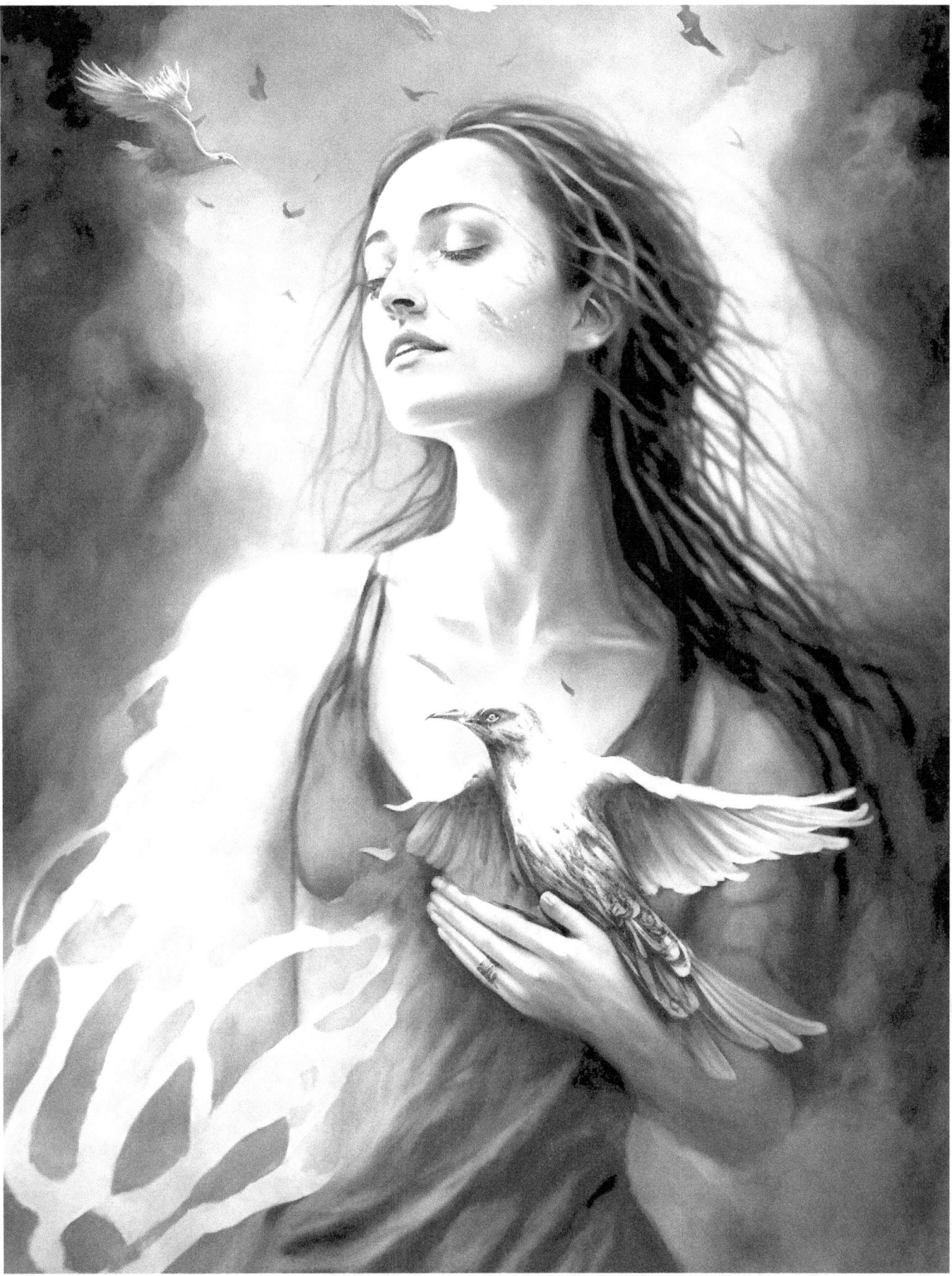

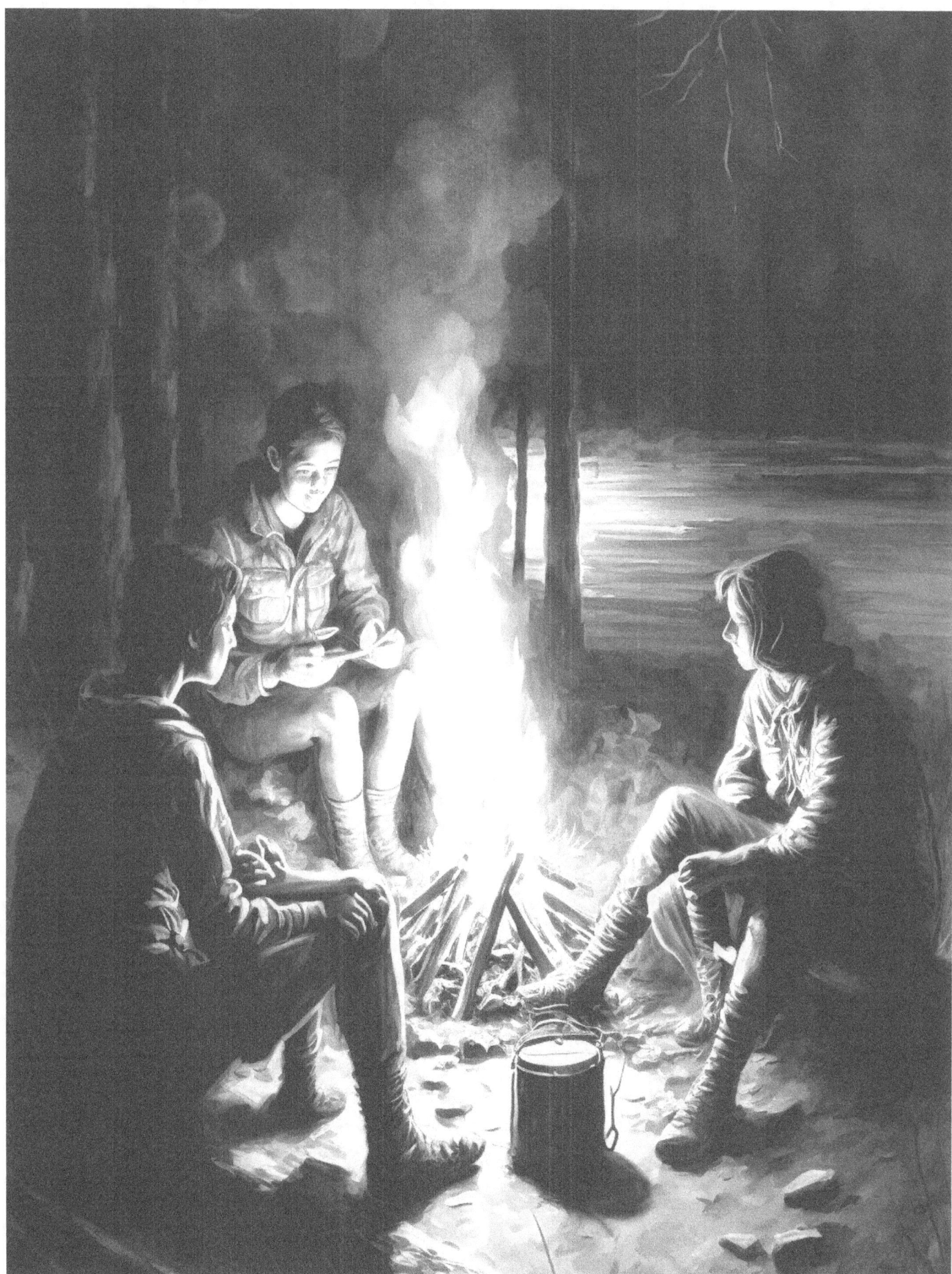

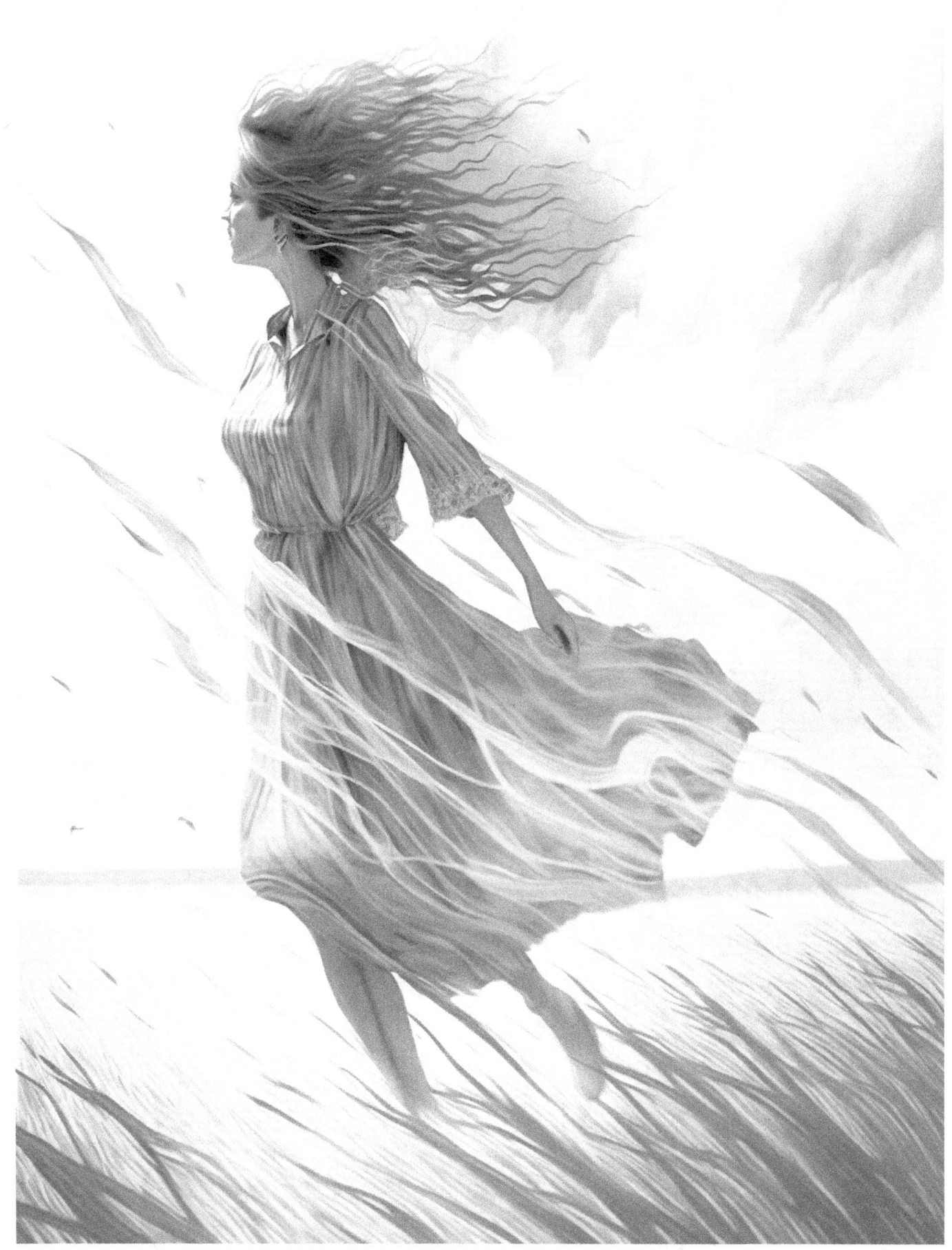

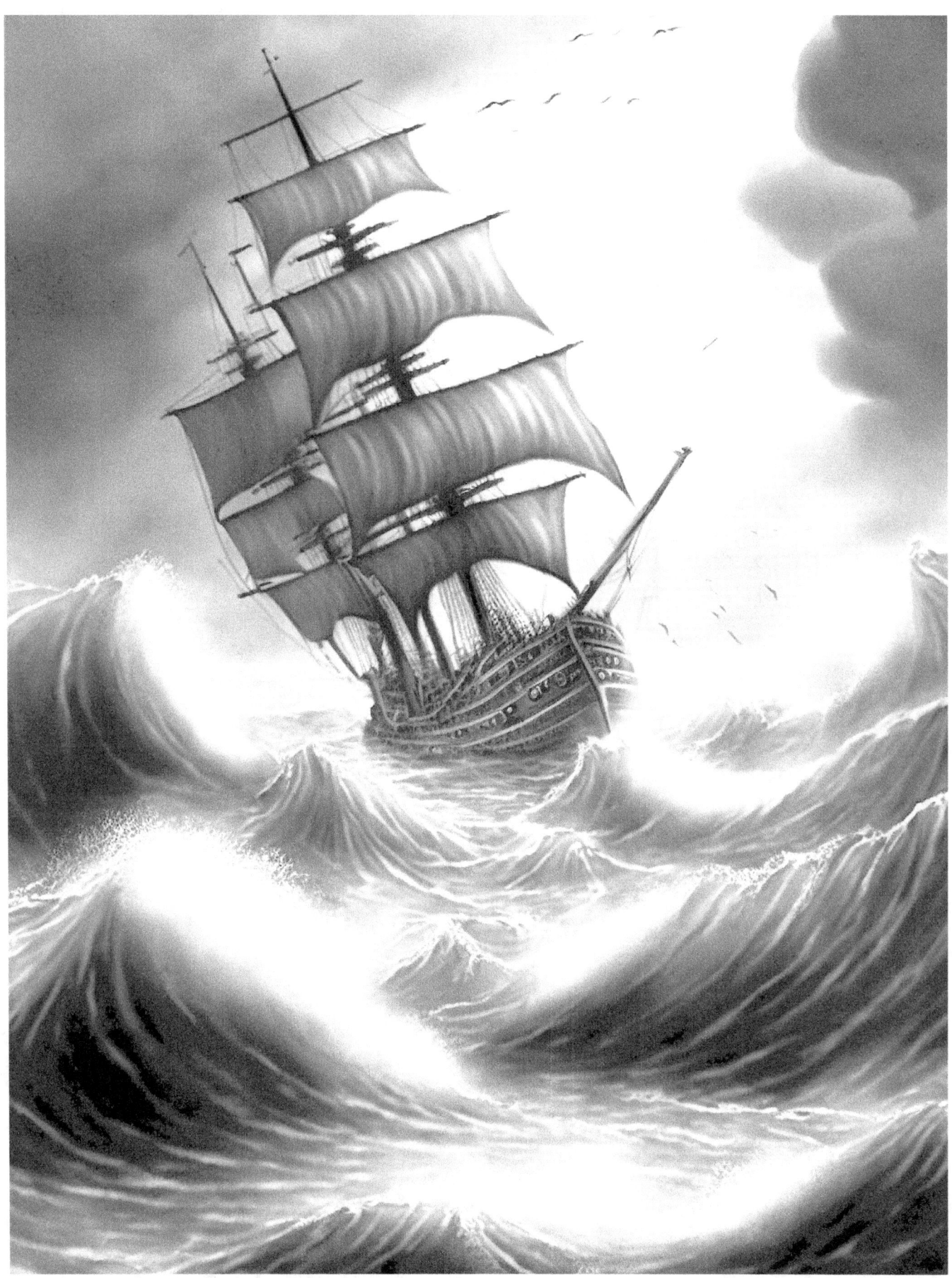

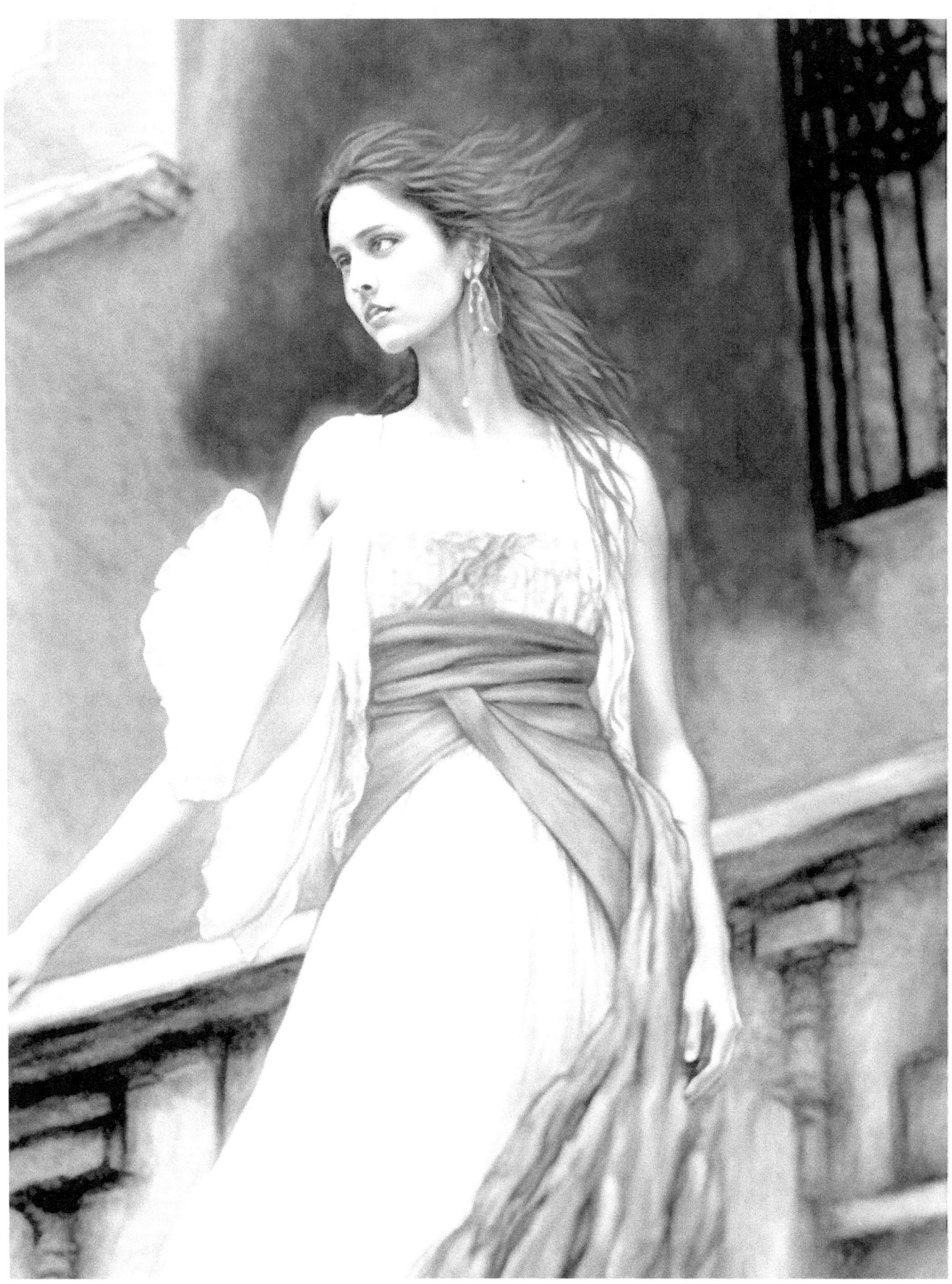

KATE TAYLOR DESING

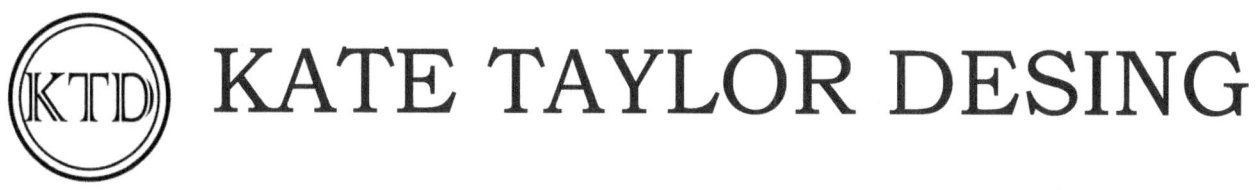

MYSTICAL CREATURES

- A Dragon Coloring Book for Adults
- A Unicorn Coloring Book for Adults
- A Phoenix Coloring Book fo Adults
- A Fairy Coloring Book for Adults
- A Mermaid Coloring Book for Adults
- A Goblin Coloring Book for Adults
- A Gnome Coloring Book for Adults
- A Troll Coloring Book for Adults
- A Gryphon Coloring Book for Adults

VEHICLES

- American muscle cars coloring book for kids
- Supercars coloring book for kids
- Antique car coloring book for kids
- Jumbo cars coloring book for kids
- Motorcycle Coloring book for kids

THE HORRORS OF COLOR

- The Dark Carnival: A Coloring Book for Adult
- The Haunted Mansion: A Coloring Book for Adults
- The Curse of the Mummy: A Coloring Book for Adults
- Nightmare Bugs: A Coloring Book for Adults
- Dark Witchcraft: A Coloring Book for Adults
- The Spectral World: A Coloring Book for Adults
- Cemetery Chronicles: A Coloring Book for Adults
- Sinister Forest: A Coloring Book for Adults
- Vampire Dreams: A Coloring Book for Adults
- Horror coloring book

MANDALAS AND PATTERNS

- Geometric shapes and patterns coloring book
- Adult coloring book tessellations patterns
- Adult coloring book geometric patterns
- Adult coloring book circular patterns.
- 150 Mandala coloring book

ARTISTIC ADVENTURES

- Surreal Escapes: A Coloring Book for Adults

- Cubist Explorations: A Coloring Book for Adults

- Impressionist Sensations: A Coloring Book for Adults

- Art Nouveau Revival: A Coloring Book for Adults

- Art Deco Magic: A Coloring Book for Adults

- Baroque Beauty: A Coloring Book for Adults

- Renaissance Reflections: A Coloring Book for Adults

- Neo Classical Nostalgia: A Coloring Book for Adults

- Romantic Visions: A Coloring Book for Adults

CHILDREN

- The Toddler Coloring Book

- Unicorn Coloring Book

- Dinosaur Coloring Book

- Mermaid Coloring Book

- Kawaii Friends Coloring Book